Using Everyday Numbers Effectively in Research

Stephen Gorard

continuum
LONDON • NEW YORK

Continuum International Publishing Group

The Tower Building　　　　　15th East 26th Street
11 York Road　　　　　　　　New York
London SE1 7NX　　　　　　　NY 10010

www.continuumbooks.com

British Library Cataloguing-in-Publication Data
A catalogue record for this book is available from the British Library.

ISBN: 0-8264-8830-7 (paperback)

Typeset by YHT Ltd, London
Printed and bound in Great Britain by MPG Books Ltd,
Bodmin, Cornwall

Using Everyday Numbers Effectively in Research

Stephen Gorard titles

Quantitative Methods in Educational Research

Quantitative Methods in Social Science Research

Continuum Research Methods Series

Action Research – Patrick Costello

Research Questions – Richard Andrews

Analysing Media Texts – Andrew Burn and David Parker

Ethics in Research – Ian Gregory

Researching Post-Compulsory Education – Jill Jameson and Yvonne Hillier

Evaluation Methods in Research – Judith Bennett

Systematic Reviews – Carol Torgerson

Using Focus Groups in Research – Lia Litosseliti

Real World Research Series

Series Editor: Bill Gillham

Developing a Questionnaire – Bill Gillham

The Research Interview – Bill Gillham

Case Study Research Methods – Bill Gillham

For my sisters: Rowena, Heather and Liz

Contents

Contents

Preface: Why This Is Not a Book About Statistics

No experience of statistics is needed to read this book, and no great knowledge of statistics will be gained by reading it. This is a book about the use of everyday numbers in research. These numbers are of the same kind as we use successfully in our everyday lives when telling the time, checking our change, catching a train, or cooking a meal. The numbers are quite straightforward, and so are the techniques we use to deal with them. These numbers have a key role to play in advancing our knowledge of education, but they are being routinely ignored by most researchers. This is partly because of a schism between those who use numbers in their research and everyone else, but it is mostly because those who *do* use numbers have elevated their work into an obscure, unrealistic, and off-putting 'paradigm' called 'quantitative research' or 'statistics'. This is *not* a book about such things, and this preface explains why.

At its simplest level, quantitative research refers to research based on evidence in the form of numbers or measurements. This is meant to distinguish it from 'qualitative' research, which is generally based on evidence in the form of texts and narratives. An analysis of the extent to which the current test scores of a group of students could be predicted by their earlier scores in similar tests would, therefore, be an example of quantitative research. Another example would be a consideration of the rates of participation in higher education by different social groups. The term quantitative research is usually to taken to refer, more narrowly, to either experimental research, or the conduct of questionnaire surveys. However, those who use this term often imply more than the simple contrast between work involving numbers and work involving narratives. In addition, much quantitative work in social science uses the techniques of 'statistics', based on a well-established theory of sampling. This emphasis on statistics is particularly prevalent in psychology, for example.

Sampling theory assumes that the measurements used by a researcher are from a subset of a larger 'population', that anyone in the larger population could have been selected for the research, and that the subset (or sample) has been selected or allocated randomly. It also assumes that the purpose of any analysis is to estimate a likelihood that the population has the same characteristics and patterns as those discovered in any sample. A further assumption is that the entire sample originally selected for inclusion in the research had agreed to take part. If these assumptions are met then researchers can calculate estimates of how much of the variability in their findings is due to the process of random sampling or allocation – using techniques such as standard errors or confidence intervals. Also, researchers can then use a significance test, such as a t-test or a chi-squared test, to help them decide whether the findings from the research sample can be safely generalized to the entire population.

An entire approach to research, sometimes referred to as a 'paradigm', has been built on this deceptively simple base. International surveys, market research, attitude and opinion scaling, laboratory experiments, and randomized field trials, are all usually considered to be conducted within this genre. In addition, many quantitative researchers move on to the field of statistical modelling, in which several measurements are combined in order to try to create an explanation for a social process. Many of these explanatory models are based on the idea of regression. Where two measurements are strongly related (such as a score on a test taken at age 11 and a later test score at age 13) then one measurement can be 'predicted' reasonably accurately from the other. In multiple regression, several measurements are used to predict the value of another.

These methods of traditional statistics can be elegant and powerful, but they are also sometimes difficult to understand. Modelling requires substantial prior knowledge of statistics to be used effectively. This means that a considerable part of beginners' training in quantitative research is based on statistics, which can be off-putting for newcomers with anxieties about mathematics. It also means that many researchers believe that this is *all* that quantitative research is, and can be. A problem for this rather narrow view of quantitative research is that much research in social science is not, in fact, based on a sample drawn randomly from a pre-defined population. The people in the selected sample rarely all agree to take part anyway, and the figures we use are never entirely accurate. In reality, most researchers work with incomplete samples selected for their own convenience, and with figures containing a hefty component of measurement error. The careful probability calculations of sampling theory do not apply in such situations. All of this means that the practice of statistics, as described above, should not be as widespread as it is. It remains popular for a variety of reasons – partly because the models that can be built on this basis are powerful and rhetorically appealing, partly because the practice is quite openly abused with unsuitable data (Shvyrkov 1997), and partly because some researchers have difficulty imagining what to do instead.

One alternative, increasing in popularity, is to perform calculations with population data instead of with samples. This is possible because of the increasing public availability of powerful datasets derived from officially collected international, national and regional statistics, or other figures originally collected for another purpose. One advantage in using population figures is that it makes the issues of generalization and significance testing, as described above, completely irrelevant. This leaves analysts with the problem of deciding whether the differences or patterns they observe in their population data are big enough to be worthy of note. Is a difference or pattern substantial enough to outweigh the potential bias caused by errors in the measurement or non-response, for example? However, exactly the same questions are faced by analysts using the traditional statistical approach – but they are usually ignored in the exclusive and blinkered concern over the variation caused by random sampling.

Research involving numbers, therefore, faces an uncertain but exciting future. It may be that new generations of researchers will begin to focus more on the kinds of real everyday numbers, such as the frequencies and true measurements described in this book, on analyses not involving random sampling, and on making subjective judgements about the importance of findings. If so, quantitative social science may cease to be considered a paradigm totally separated from qualitative research, cease to be considered so mathematically threatening to outsiders, and so be more open to work that mixes data of all kinds in searching for solutions to important problems for society.

In summary, here is a simple checklist for potential researchers to follow in deciding whether to use the approaches described in this book, or whether to use a traditional statistics book instead.

1. Do you genuinely want to find something out?
   If NO then do not consider doing any research, put the book down and pick a different occupation instead.

2. Are you determined to ignore potentially important information for your research merely because it appears in numeric form?
   If YES then put the book down, you are a 'quali-wally' and probably lied in your answer to question 1.

3. Are you working with a sample of cases selected (or allocated) randomly from a larger pre-defined population all of whom could have been selected for the research?
   If NO then you cannot use traditional statistical techniques such as standard errors or significance tests, so buy and read *this* book instead.

4. Will you get full response from your chosen random sample (i.e. no one refusing to take part and no missing data for any reason)?
   If NO then be aware that traditional statistical techniques can do nothing to compensate for these problems, so buy and read *this* book.

5. Will the numbers you use come from counting or measuring things without any error (i.e. will your measurements be perfect representations of what you are studying)?
   If NO then be aware that traditional statistical techniques only address variation stemming from your random sampling and do nothing to address the problem of measurement error, therefore buy and read *this* book.

6. Will your study be otherwise free from error in recording and transcription, so that there is no error component that could increase through propagation as the computer conducts your complex statistical calculations?

If YES then you probably misunderstood the questions so far (in which case, try again).

If NO then buy and read *this* book at once.

The examples used in the book are drawn largely from research in education, my own field, but the ideas they are used to illustrate apply to all of the social sciences more generally.

List of figures

List of tables

1

Introducing Everyday Numbers

'Statistics are no substitute for judgement'
Henry Clay (1777–1852)

Introduction

We all use numbers every day of our lives. We tell the time and date, and plan meetings or lectures, or we arrange our travel to work, conferences and holidays. We look at dials and digital displays concerning fuel, car speed, stock market indices, battery life and fridge temperature. We shop, compare prices, check our change and pay bills. We watch television involving numbers on the weather forecast, as scores on games shows and quizzes, and measurements for history, archaeology or home improvement programmes. Even the channels on television are represented as numbers and tuning frequencies. We programme the video or DVD recorder. We send text messages or telephone to a 'number'. Our digital cameras, radios, games consoles and computers are based entirely on numbers (or digits). We weigh, measure by eye, and combine ingredients in cooking, and in decorating and DIY. We may check our weight, our partners' temperature, or our children's foot size. We may play cards, darts, or musical instruments. Numbers are far

1

from the most important things in our lives but, on the other hand, our lives would be harder to organize and impoverished by their absence. Everyone uses numbers in their everyday lives to some extent, and most people use them quite unproblematically. Obviously, people miss meetings, overcook the pasta, record the wrong television programme and so on. But they generally know, or quickly learn, how the various numbering systems work, and how to manipulate them with relative ease. Most people will successfully record, process and output a phenomenal amount of numeric information every day.

What a contrast there is with our behaviour in social science research! The same people who can calculate the score for a break in snooker, fill in a hire-purchase form, control a research budget, or check a lecture timetable, suddenly say that they have no skill in using numbers for research. In their view, the numbers involved in research behave very differently and are much more complicated than the numbers they deal with routinely elsewhere. This is *not* so. Every researcher can and should use numbers in their research. As with everyday life, numbers are not the most important things in research, but our research findings are impoverished by their absence. This book seeks to remedy the situation by illustrating how the kind of simple numeric techniques we use every day are of considerable value in research as well, and how ignoring these techniques often leads researchers into error and fallacy. In the final chapter, the book also looks at one of the reasons why so many researchers end up with this peculiar separation between their numeric common sense and the (non-) use of numbers in their research. This reason is the wholly unnecessary complexity of techniques and training for traditional statistics.

There is little social science research that routinely uses 'everyday' numeric evidence, partly because there are so few researchers prepared to work with numbers of any kind (Rendall 2003). A variety of reasons can be suggested for this situation. It might stem from researchers' off-putting experiences of mathematics at school, leading to generally negative attitudes towards 'academic' numeric issues, and relatively low levels of numeracy among social science students. In fact, Meehl (1998) suggests that there can be considerable self-selection for poor ability with numbers among students electing to study social science subjects. Perhaps the ability of social science students is also generally weaker, in comparison to students in science and the humanities, and this simply becomes more apparent when dealing with numbers, which can have a right and wrong solution, rather than text and pictures, which generally do not (Onwuegbuzie and Wilson 2003). This weakness may be reinforced by poor teaching at university level, and a lack of perceived relevance to the students' own practice (Murtonen and Lehtinen 2003). Students in social science now dread their compulsory statistics courses, which are always reported as the most anxiety-inducing. Most complete their obligatory methods training at both undergraduate and postgraduate level successfully, but come away confused by the idea of 'statistics'. Too often their own assumption, and that of their trainers, is that the 'blame' lies mainly with them. This is also *not* so. In fact, the main reason that newcomers are put off using numbers in their research is that 'statistics' is made so unnecessarily scary by its advocates.

Very little of the content in introductory statistics courses is about everyday numbers, what these numbers represent, and how useful they are (or are not) as theoretical models of the underlying research situation. Instead, students are quickly introduced to probability theory, and the complex pattern of analysis and modelling built upon it. The problem is that many novices will just as quickly see that this whole superstructure is built on very impractical foundations. Why should they learn something as complicated as this when they are unlikely ever to use it in practice? Look at some of the assumptions underlying the mathematics of probability testing and modelling as if you were reading them for the first time. Try not to be scared by them. Note, instead, how ridiculous they are:

1. The sample must be selected (or allocated) randomly from a known population. By way of illustration, none of the articles in the *British Educational Research Journal* (*BERJ*) in 2002 met this assumption, whether they used statistics or not (Gorard *et al.* 2004a).

2. The sample must be complete, with full response and no respondent dropout. None of the articles in *BERJ* in 2002 met this assumption either.

3. The measurements involved must be made without error. This assumption is mathematically convenient, but clearly inappropriate for social research. The assumption is sometimes defended by claiming that minor initial errors lead to only minor errors in conclusions. But the most common statistical procedures are in fact 'excessively sensitive to seemingly minor deviations' (Huber 1981, p. 1).

4. The measurements involved are often expected to follow an ideal distribution, such as the normal, or Gaussian, curve. In practice, even on those rare occasions when the data *do* approximate this ideal distribution, they tend to be 'longer-tailed', containing more of the extreme values than the ideal. In practice, this fact is often obscured by the dishonest deletion of these inconvenient values (in Barnett and Lewis 1978).

These assumptions clearly do not apply to our use of numbers in everyday life. But these four assumptions and others like them are so unrealistic that no study in social science research will meet them either. Logically, this means that no analysis based on them could ever be justified. So why bother with them? Given all of this, it is clear why the majority of new researchers do not bother to learn about the more complex forms of analysis and modelling built on this rather shaky foundation. And yet, working with numbers in research does not have to be complicated or unrealistic, any more than working with everyday numbers does. Using everyday number techniques in research is easy. It can lead to very important research discoveries, and injects a necessary dose of critical realism into claims based on more complex approaches. This book illustrates each of these three claims.

Using Everyday Numbers Is Easy

To a large extent, a book explaining to most readers how to use numbers in research in the same way as they do in their everyday lives is not needed. Since most people are perfectly competent already, what could the book teach them? Partly, this book provides a defence against any commentators who might say that everyday numbers and the techniques associated with them are not suitable for use in research – the statistical fundamentalists. This defence is partly provided throughout, but it is the main focus of Chapter 3. Partly, this book also provides examples of research involving the simple use of numbers (and no statistics). Such examples appear in this chapter and the next. These illustrate the basic techniques that can be used, the importance of the kinds of results that emerge from such simple considerations of patterns, and the crucial ways in which misleading research findings have previously emerged, in practice, when such apparently simple issues have been ignored.

The techniques themselves are rather easy, consisting of primary school arithmetic and no mathematics. Counting and measuring, adding and subtracting, converting to percentages, and presenting simple tables and graphs are all that is required. Many of the everyday activities discussed at the start of the chapter, which you already perform successfully, are much more sophisticated than the examples given in this book. For a more detailed discussion of the very simple approaches to numeric analysis see Gorard (2003a, Chapter 2).

Simple Figures

The basis of all numeric work is, of course, the simple figure or measurement. It should be expressed in such a way as to make clear the units of measurement, its source and any key characteristics. According to the Employers' Organisation (2002), for example, resignations by school teachers in England and Wales totalled 47,930 in 2001. This is quite clear and straightforward. The more precise definitions of 'teachers' (does it include sixth form lecturers?), resignations (does it include those moving to a different teaching post?), 'England and Wales', and when in 2001 the census was taken, are all explained in the reference given. These definitions will be particularly important if we subsequently wish to compare this simple figure with an apparently equivalent figure taken from another year or another country. The figure itself could be a sum found by adding a set of other numbers, such as the number of teachers resigning for different reasons including age, ill-health, and moving to a different occupation. You could create this total, using your primary school arithmetic skills, or with a calculator or spreadsheet. In creating, and quoting, such a simple figure you will have performed a useful numeric analysis. To do this you do *not* need to consider any philosophical issues, such as the paradigm in which you are working, any more than you would when doing a calculation in real life (Gorard 2004a, 2004b). There is no necessary entailment from epistemology to specific research methods (Johnson and Onwuegbuzie 2004). In this example, there is no sample, and so no role for significance tests, confidence intervals, standard errors and the remaining panoply of traditional statistical approaches.

A simple figure such as the number of teachers resigning each year can be expressed as itself – a 'frequency', or how frequent resignation is. Simple figures are also commonly expressed as a proportion of something else, such as the number of teachers resigning divided by the total number of teachers. If there were, for the sake of argument, 274,286 teachers in England and Wales in 2001, then the resignations divided by the total produces the answer 0.17474461 (using my calculator). It is very important, at this point, that you do not succumb to the same kind of claim to spurious accuracy that abounds in most statistical reports. The final digit (1) in the number 0.17474461 represents the fractional number one hundred millionth (or 1 over 100,000,000). If you quote this figure, then you are claiming that you can count the proportion of resignations to that level of accuracy. But there are only 274,286 teachers in total. To use a figure of one hundred millionth implies that you are measuring resignations to the nearest four hundredth of a teacher! In everyday life the concept of a four hundredth of a teacher would sound like complete nonsense. It *is* nonsense – in everyday life, and in research for the same reasons. Trust your instinct here. This means that you are being rhetorically dishonest if you quote the final digit (1) in your research report, because you are suggesting a level of accuracy in your results that is unattainable. But the same argument applies to the second to last digit (6) as well, and so on. In fact, when you consider that there are likely to be errors in the recording of both the number of teachers and their resignations, you can see that it is best to be conservative about the accuracy of your proportion.

Perhaps rounding the calculated answer to 0.17 is appropriate, which is both easier for others to read (i.e. more democratic) and it only suggests accuracy to the nearest one hundredth of the 47,930 resigning teachers, or around 500 teachers – a perfectly proper real-life number of teachers. Put another way, we would have ended up with the same answer of 0.17 even if the number of resigning teachers had been anything from near 47,430 to near 48,430. Therefore, our result allows for a realistic level of measurement, transcription and non-response errors (see Chapter 2). To imply greater accuracy than this, as is standard practice in traditional statistical reports, is not justified.

This kind of proportion is most commonly expressed as a percentage, or number in every hundred, by multiplying it by one hundred. In our example, 0.17 is the same as 17 per cent. So we could say that 17 per cent of serving teachers in England and Wales resigned in 2001. Percentages are thought to be an easy-to-comprehend way of expressing proportions. They are helpful when there are only one or two sets of percentages, as here. As this book illustrates later, complications arise when several percentages are in play at once, and I recommend that you work with the original frequencies and create your own proportions from these whenever possible.

Comparisons

Perhaps the next most basic element in numeric analysis is the comparison, without calculation, between a series of two or more numbers. For example, our figure of 17 per cent teacher resignations can be compared with the equivalent for other years to see whether such resignations have increased or decreased over time. The comparison would simply be of the size of the two numbers. Of course, there will be vital issues to consider when making a claim that resignations have grown (or not). Do the figures concerned all use the same definition of 'resignation', are their sources and methods of collection the same, and what is their likely measurement error and non-response bias? You should clarify all such issues as far as possible before making a tentative decision about the relevance of differences between two figures. Given the likely inaccuracies in the figures we might decide that a figure of 18 per cent for 2002 is not substantially different from 17 per cent. However, a figure of 40 per cent for 2002 would imply a change in the recorded level of resignations that would clearly require some considerable explanation.

When there are more than two figures to compare, such as when looking at extended differences over time or space, then a simple table can be a useful summary. If generated by software, the table should be shorn of irrelevant or confusing labels and information, and you, rather than the software, should decide the number of decimal places to present. Remember also to set the left/right justification so that digits with the same value are in the same position in each table cell. As an example, Table 1.1 shows the total number of advertised vacancies for secondary school teachers in Wales over six academic

Table 1.1 *Teacher vacancies in secondary schools, Wales, 1996/97 to 2001/02*

Year	1996/97	1997/98	1998/99	1999/00	2000/01	2001/02
Vacancies	38	60	77	42	60	77

Source: Form Stats 3 (formerly 618G)

years. These represent unfilled teaching posts of at least one term's duration, as advertised by Welsh secondary schools in that year. The table has a heading that tries to be as informative as possible (the what, where and when), and a footnote giving some information about the source. The form STATS 3 (cited in the footnote) is part of the January annual schools census, rather like the Form 7 completed by all schools in England. Therefore, the vacancy rate is a 'snapshot' of the posts unfilled at the time of the census. A footnote is also a good place to give further detailed information about one or more cells – if the method of collecting teacher vacancy data changed in 2001, for example. The first row in the table shows the academic year, and the second gives the number of vacancies as a series of simple figures.

What can we conclude from Table 1.1? There is no obvious trend over time. While negative and rather basic, such an observation should not be dismissed lightly. This is important. Imagine, instead, that the figure for each year was slightly higher than the previous one. Even though the annual difference may be small (too small to be 'detected' by traditional statistical approaches), a sequence of small growths taken as a *whole* can be pretty convincing, and call for an explanation. So, the fact that we do not have such a sequence here is equally important. Because the numbers involved are small, it is quite likely that the annual changes represent little more than the volatility of small numbers, and the sum of many individuals' decisions and opportunities. The annual differences are even smaller than the already small vacancy figures. Natural volatility, therefore, provides us with a good plausible interpretation of the changes. The lack of a sequence also allows us to gainsay anyone claiming that vacancies have been growing steadily over time (as they might appear to if we only considered the years 1999/00 to 2001/02).

However, it is still worth giving some attention to other features of the table. Why are the figures lower in 1996/97 and 1999/00? Why does a pattern of growth appear to repeat after three years? Questions such as these cannot be answered by the data in Table 1.1. This is another difference between everyday approaches and traditional statistics. In the latter, datasets are routinely used to generate patterns, and then tested for an explanation using the *same* dataset. One of the ways in which we could seek an explanation for the apparent cycle in Table 1.1 is to use data from other years – either by trawling back through archives or by waiting for successive years. If the figure for 1995/96 was 40 and the figure for 2002/03 was 63 then our three-year cycle is well and truly broken. Probably the most fruitful way to seek an explanation is to look for different kinds of data. Policy documents and financial statements from each year, for example, could help explain variation in the demand for teachers. If schools in Wales were given a substantial increase in funding in 2001, then this could explain the increased demand for teachers in January 2002. Using everyday numbers in research leads, almost inevitably, to such combined methods approaches (Gorard with Taylor 2004). It also leads, quite naturally, to the generation of several different plausible explanations of any phenomena. Although anathema to many researchers, who may wish to make bolder claims, it should be clear that any data pattern is capable of such multiple explanations. In fact, any data pattern will probably *have* multiple explanations. Our job, as researchers, is partly a creative one of generating the most plausible explanations, and partly a logical one of grading or rejecting them. This mixture of imagination and logical analysis is integral to all good scientific research (Phillips 1999, Gorard 2002a).

In our present state of ignorance in social science, what the simple use of everyday numbers can do is eliminate at the outset any 'explanations' that do not fit what we do know. If the figures in Table 1.1 are for the only years available, then we would reject any 'explanation' of why vacancies in Wales are growing continuously over time. The explanation must be wrong because what it purports to explain is not actually happening. Education research, in particular, is rife with such fake explanations drawn from small-scale work that pays no attention at all to the numeric patterns the explanations pretend to address. This is one of the prices we pay as a field for the non-sensical division of methods into 'paradigms' (Gorard 2004a).

While such simple figures as those dealt with so far are more useful than many readers might imagine, we will often wish to look at the types and categories *within* our headline figures in more detail. Table 1.2 differs from Table 1.1 in being two-dimensional. It is really just a set of seven tables like Table 1.1, each showing a series of figures over time. Each row can be read independently. But, for convenience of comparison, and to avoid repeating the first row seven times, the seven tables are run together. The same comments as made above about the title, simplicity, formatting and footnotes still apply. Note that by right-justifying the main cells, the single-digit

Table 1.2 *Pupil-to-teacher ratios, schools in Wales by type, 1996/97 to 2000/01*

Year	1996/97	1997/98	1998/99	1999/00	2000/01
Nursery	19	18	18	17	17
Primary	23	23	22	22	22
Secondary	16	17	17	17	17
Special	7	7	7	7	7
All maintained	19	20	19	19	19
Independent	10	10	10	10	10
Overall	19	19	19	19	18

Source: Schools in Wales – General Statistics 2001

figure for special schools becomes aligned with the units in the two-digit figures for the other types of schools. The cells contain a proportion calculated by dividing the total number of pupils by the number of teachers, for each type of school. This is known as the pupil-to-teacher ratio (PTR). So, in special schools there are, understandably, only seven pupils for each teacher on average. In primary schools, there are over 20 pupils per teacher. Although the actual PTRs are necessarily small, they represent in each case an index of hundreds of teachers and thousands of pupils. Given this, and their near constancy over time, we may conclude that the variations between school types are not simply due to the vagaries of small numbers. There is evidence here of design.

Perhaps the most interesting point to observe about Table 1.2 is, again, a negative one. There are few changes of any substance over time. More importantly, even the very small changes one could arguably identify are downward, leading to smaller PTRs. This is important because these years represent a period when teaching in Wales was said to be in crisis, with so few teachers that some schools had to close temporarily or for one or more days every week (see below). Whatever the crisis was, the figures here show that it was not due to the overall number of teachers in proportion to the number of pupils.

I find tables of simple figures extremely useful and informative, and I believe that the main reason why people get put off reading tables is the discourtesy of those authors who publish tables of many dimensions with technical clutter, unintelligible labels, and figures to seven decimal places. A significance test cannot be used with the kind of data in Table 1.2, which is from a census and not a random sample (see Chapter 3). Therefore, the table does not require probabilities, asterisks showing alpha levels, or unhelpful numbers based on the 't' or 'F' distributions, for example. I might have used abbreviated variable names or column headings when entering the data into analytical software, but I assume that the reader does not wish to know what these were. Therefore, the rows are labelled 'Nursery' or 'Independent' rather than 'NSY' or 'IDT'. I have already dealt with the spurious accuracy implied by repeating the set number of decimal places generated automatically by a computer or calculator. Shorn of such nonsense, tables should be easy to read. If they are not, then the responsibility lies, in the first instance, with the table author rather than their readers. Because tables are so easy to use, and they present the actual figures, I prefer them to graphs. However, there are occasions when a graph makes a nice narrative touch.

Figure 1.1 shows the kind of simple numbers that could be presented as a table, but which make a reasonably clear graphic as well. It shows the proportion (percentage) of all teachers in England and Wales who have

Figure 1.1 *Wastage rates (per cent) for full-time teachers, England and Wales, 1989/90 to 1999/2000*

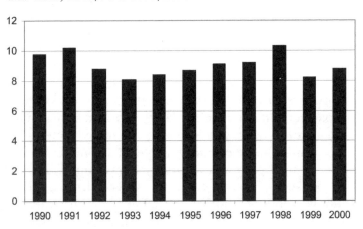

Source: DfES, Database of Teacher Records.

14

apparently left the teaching profession in each year from 1989/90 to 1999/2000. Note that the same consideration should be given to graphs as to tables – source of data, footnoted interpretations, lack of clutter, meaningful header, and so on. Although a graph like this means that the reader cannot now see the actual figures per year, for some readers the graph makes it easier to see the trend over time, and the relative scale of any changes between years. What could we conclude from Figure 1.1?

As with tables, it is important to know as much as possible about the genesis of the figures involved, especially concerning any changes in definition or collection over time. One relevant factor to know here is that the data at source are accompanied by a warning that 'the wastage rate for those aged 50 and over in 1997 and 1998 reflects the increase in early retirements brought about by changes to the Teachers' Pension Scheme in April 1997 and September 1997. The subsequent decrease in early retirements resulted in a much lower wastage rate in 1999'. Once this important caveat has been taken into account, there are no particularly remarkable trends in the wastage rates. Although the proportion of teachers leaving the profession rose year-on-year from 1993 to 1997, the change in legislation affecting figures after 1997 obscures the extent to which this may, or may not, have continued over the following two years. At the end of this sequence, when wastage reached a peak in 1998 it was still only at the same level as wastage in 1990/91. We cannot conclude that, overall, more (or fewer) teachers are leaving the profession over time.

I still believe that a table of the figures is as easy to read as the graph in Figure 1.1, and more informative as well. However, a simple chart does no harm. A big problem with graphs lies in the range and sophistication available via software such as Excel or SPSS, and also in the software's default settings. These options often make graphs very hard to understand, and so play a similar role to the default settings of calculator software when generating impenetrable variable names or an automatic eight decimal places. In repeating these defaults in their reports, authors inadvertently make their reports harder to understand, and reinforce the prejudices of those who 'don't do numbers'. Pie charts, 3D graphs, obscure 'legends', and two or more graphs in one, are all examples that are generally misused.

When considering using a graph, remember two key points. Your objective is to make things easier to understand – so as a rule of thumb if the graph requires considerable explanation as well, it is probably a red herring. The main point you are making via the graph should be obvious to all at first glance, even if the point you are making is that there is no pattern, or no change. Second, you are supposed to be in control of the software, which is in turn meant to make it easier for you to draw graphs. So if the graph you end up with is not what you planned then learn more about the software, change your software, draw your graphs in some other way, or simply do not use the graph. A particular problem is the use of line graphs, where the software plots the figures as points and draws a line between each figure in the series. Consider what the line itself represents. Figure 1.1, for example, could have been drawn in this way, and the lines between years would have implied that the annual changes were taking place continuously and smoothly. But we have no evidence that this is so. A line graph would not be completely inappropriate here, but would not add much clarity and might be misleading. Where the figures in a series have no clear temporal order, a line graph is almost always inappropriate.

Mean and Mean Deviation

The final part of this section looks at averages and variation around an average, from the perspective of everyday numbers. Most standard texts introduce the reader to a range of different averages, and of ways of assessing variation around an average. Here, we shall focus on only one average – the mean – and one form of variation – the mean deviation. Having explained averages such as the mode (most frequently occurring figure) and the median (middle of a series of figures in order), standard texts anyway tend then to focus only on the mean, which is the everyday average. The mean is so well known as the average in everyday situations that most non-research reports do not bother to specify it. The mean average of a set of figures is simply the sum of all of the figures in the set divided by the number of figures.

If you are in a restaurant with a group of friends, you may decide to share the bill at your table by dividing the total cost by the number of people. This is usually easier and less embarrassing than itemizing who ate and drank what. It is fair, provided no one was outrageously extravagant, and probably works out even in the long run anyway. When people do this they are calculating a 'mean' average. *Everyone* knows how to do it, even though we all make mistakes (perhaps especially after a meal). But students get confused after exposure to the kinds of methods, courses and texts that insist on muddling up the mean with the largely unused alternative averages, and with the much more complex issue of the distribution of the figures themselves (see Chapter 3). Like most everyday uses of numbers in research, you already know how to do it and have sound views on when using the mean average is and is not appropriate. Have confidence, think 'average', think 'restaurant'.

I suggested in the last paragraph that the mean, as used

in sharing a restaurant bill, is appropriate when most people at the table have spent similar amounts. I suggest also that most readers will have understood what I meant by this. Therefore, most already have a grasp of the idea that is technically expressed as variation around the mean, or, more simply, as how much each figure in a set of figures tends to differ from all of the others. For the restaurant example, we could work out this variation. Imagine that there are eight adults at the table, and the actual cost of each person's meal, in local currency, is:

13, 10, 12, 11, 8, 6, 12, and 8.

The average cost to be paid by each person is the total bill:

13 + 10 + 12 + 11 + 8 + 6 + 12 + 8 equals 80

divided by the number of people:

80 / 8 equals 10.

So everyone pays 10.

The first person, in fact, pays 3 too little, the second is spot on, the third pays 2 too little and so on. Clearly the sum of all these deviations from the average is going to be zero. The sum of 3, 0, 2, 1, −2, −4, 2, and −2 is, indeed, zero. What we need to do to find the average amount by which each person's cost deviates from the mean is to ignore the direction of the difference (the + and − signs), add the differences together and divide by the number of people:

3 + 0 + 2 + 1 + 2 + 4 + 2 + 2 equals 16.

Divided by the number of people:

16 / 8 equals 2.

We have found the mean deviation of the cost to be 2,

around the mean cost of 10. The mean deviation is a useful summary of the variability in a set of figures. In a sense, it tells us how representative the mean of the figures is, or in terms of the example it tells us how fair it is that everybody at the table pays the same. Where the mean deviation is large in comparison to the mean, then the mean is not very representative of the whole set of figures (because they vary widely). Perhaps, in that case, a different way of dividing the bill would be fairer. If the mean deviation is small in comparison to the mean, as it is in this example, then the mean is a good representation of the set of figures. If the mean deviation is near zero then most figures are at or very near the mean – there is almost no variability.

Traditional texts either do not describe this simple mean deviation or else describe it briefly and then recommend the use of several alternatives instead. The most commonly proposed alternative is called the 'standard deviation', which has several disadvantages compared to the mean deviation in being harder to calculate, not having a clear everyday meaning, and over-emphasizing extreme scores (see Chapter 3). You may also have encountered inter-quartile ranges, stem and leaf plots, or box and whisker plots, suggested to help show the variability or distribution of a set of figures. Like pie-charts, 3D graphs, line graphs, the mode, median, and standard deviation, these techniques have some limited value in quite specific cases. However, they are not generally useful enough in relation to their complexity for an everyday analyst to use at this stage. Simple figures, series, cross-tabulations of series, bar graphs, ratios or proportions, percentages, means and mean deviations are just about all of the techniques that the everyday analyst needs to conduct real research.

Having outlined the kinds of techniques involved in using everyday numbers in research, this section considers a simple example of real research that was conducted, peer-reviewed, published and influential, but which used only these techniques. The example re-assesses the supposed crisis in teacher supply in the UK around the turn of the century.

Discoveries Using Everyday Techniques 1: Do We Have Enough Teachers?

A recent study, that involved nothing more than everyday numbers, set out to calculate whether there was at that time a shortage of teachers in the UK and, indeed, how we can ever decide whether there are enough teachers (see, for example, See *et al.* 2004, White *et al.* 2005, and Gorard *et al.* 2006).

At the end of the 1990s and in the early 2000s, politicians, media commentators and researchers all combined to claim that there was a serious shortage of qualified teachers in the UK. Policy-makers reported an increase in the number of designated shortage subjects, so much so that most curriculum subjects were designated shortage areas (School Teachers' Review Body, 2001). These included Welsh, ICT, geography, religious education, art, music and English, as well as the more usual maths, science and technology (School Teachers' Review Body, 2002). Local authorities reported rising numbers of vacancies for jobs, and of teacher resignations. According to a *Guardian* survey, official figures from 100 education authorities showed that vacancies amounted to 3,500 full-time posts (Smithers 2001a). Government statistics showed an alarming growth in the proportion of teachers in the secondary sector who were leaving for other employment, so that more teachers were reported to be leaving than entering teaching in 1999. There were too many 'underqualified' teachers (Levenson, 2001, Report of Sir Gareth Roberts' Review 2002), and the quality of new entrants to teaching was too low (BBC News 2001a).

Comments to the media from the Chief Inspector of Schools in England, for 2001, suggested that the teacher 'shortage' was the worst for nearly 40 years (BBC News 2001b). Headlines appeared in the *Times Educational Supplement (TES)* proclaiming that the 'Country has run out of teachers' (Dean 2000) and that, 'Staff crisis worsens as thousands quit' (Dean 2001). Published stories included: schools being forced to go on four-day weeks (Woodward 2001), pupils being sent home because there were no teachers (Hutchins 2001), recruitment for initial training failing to meet targets (Schoolsnet 2001), teachers leaving in droves (House of Commons Hansard Debates 2000) and heads relying on foreign teachers with poor command of English (Smithers 2001b). The teaching population was, apparently, ageing, so leading to a retirement 'timebomb' (Howson 2001).

All of these claims about shortages of teacher supply can be tested, to some extent, simply by looking at the patterns in the relevant publicly available official figures. Of course, these figures may be inaccurate and even misleading in some respects (bias must be presumed to be present in *all* data, after all). However, they are based on a population census, minimizing the bias caused by sampling, and they are officially collected, minimizing the bias caused by non-response or drop out. Above all, it must be recalled that the kinds of claims for a crisis cited above are not based on some superior kind of evidence. Some are based on very small-scale studies, some on anecdote or speculation, and some on the same kinds of figures as presented below. The key issue here lies not in the techniques used for analysing the numbers, but the extent to which the crisis account was warranted by the evidence that was available.

Data for the analysis below (conducted with colleagues)

21

was taken from a variety of official sites and sources, including DfES Statistics of Education: Teachers in England 2002, DfES Class Sizes and Pupil:Teacher Ratios in England 2002, the School Teachers' Review Body Statistical Annex (2000) and the School Teachers' Review Body Eleventh Report (2002), The Graduate Teacher Training Registry (GTTR) which provided *Annual Statistical Reports* from 2000 and 2001: www.gttr.ac.uk, and the Office for National Statistics (ONS): www.statistics.gov.uk.

The emphasis here is on secondary school teachers in Wales. Key figures available include:

- The number of teachers in post, broken down by sector, age, sex, subject, region, and so on.
- The number of teachers leaving full-time service in each year, and the number of teachers leaving their current school, broken down in the same way.
- The number of trainee teachers, broken down in the same way.
- The number of advertised vacancies for teaching posts of one term or more.
- The number of schools and pupils.

I have written elsewhere about some of the specific limitations of these figures, such as changes in definition, or in methods of collection or coverage over time (Gorard *et al.* 2006). The most reliable and useful figures are those for the numbers of schools, teachers and pupils. Teacher wastage and turnover figures can be misleading. They include teachers moving between the home countries of the UK, even though a teacher moving from England to Wales, for example, is not really 'wastage'. They include teachers moving from one sector to another, even though a teacher moving from a secondary school to a sixth-form college, for example, is not wastage. Turnover between schools could be interpreted as a sign of a healthy profession rather than a crisis, but high turnover tends to

Table 1.3 *Number of full-time equivalent pupils and teachers, maintained secondary schools, Wales, 1996/97 to 2000/2001*

	1996/97	1997/98	1998/99	1999/00	2000/01
Pupils	200,288	201,852	204,158	207,916	210,396
Teachers	12,397	12,228	12,384	12,471	12,692
PTR	16	17	17	17	17

Adapted from: Schools in Wales: General Statistics 2001

lead to high vacancy rates. Advertised teacher vacancy rates can, therefore, also be misleading. In an era of increased funding for education, more posts tend to be created, leading to more vacancies. Again, therefore, a high vacancy rate can be indicative of a healthy and growing profession rather than of hard-to-fill posts.

Table 1.3 shows the number of full-time (or equivalent) pupils and teachers in secondary schools in Wales from 1996/97 to 2000/2001. The final row shows the other two series as a proportion – the pupil-to-teacher ratio (PTR). It shows that the number of pupils increased every year (a quite convincing trend), but that the number of teachers also increased in proportion so that the PTR remained at about the same level. These are some of the figures that made up Table 1.2 above. We can conclude from these figures that whatever crisis the media, policy-makers and some academics were reporting it was not caused by an overall shortage of teachers in relation to the number of pupils. A similar picture emerges for England (See *et al.* 2004). By comparison, OECD (2000) figures show that secondary PTRs in Wales were considerably lower than most developed and developing countries, including Canada (22), New Zealand (21), Korea (23) and the Netherlands (19).

We have already seen from Table 1.1 that there is also no obvious trend in vacancies that can explain the 'crisis' in teacher supply. The highest recorded figure for vacancies in Wales was in 1990/91, long before the subsequent crisis, but when vacancies were five times as high as later in the decade. Again the figures for England, while higher, tell a similar story. In 1999 there were a reported 16,000 trained teachers registered as seeking jobs in England and Wales, and many more were unemployed but not receiving Jobseeker's Allowance. Even more trained teachers were in alternative employment but would have preferred to be teaching (*TES* 2002). The problem of vacancies, if there was one, could only be one of regional and subject dispersion, rather than total numbers.

Areas with higher teacher vacancy figures, such as Inner and Outer London and South-east England, operate with correspondingly low pupil-teacher ratios but (paradoxically) larger class sizes (See *et al.* 2004). Areas with low teacher vacancies, such as North-east and South-west England, operate with higher ratios but smaller class sizes. This shows that neither vacancy rates nor pupil–teacher ratios are good indicators in themselves of class size, or of a shortage of teachers. The relationship between the three depends to a large extent on the local organization of schools and the nature of their pupil and teacher intake. Areas with apparently the greatest unmet demand for teachers, such as London, actually have more teachers per pupil than anywhere else in the UK.

The number of teacher posts in any school is, in part, dependent on how many teachers the school can afford to pay for, while the number of posts altogether depends on the number of schools. Table 1.4 shows how the funding-per-pupil changed between 1995/96 and 2000/01 for maintained secondary schools in England. Funding-per-pupil fell between 1995 and 1997, the period of lowest teacher vacancies. From 1996 to 2001 pupil funding continued to increase. This coincided with the period when teacher vacancies started to rise. Vacancies are

Table 1.4 *Changes in funding per pupil in England 1995/96 to 1999/2000*

Year	1995/96	1996/97	1997/98	1998/99	1999/00	2000/01
Real-terms index	100	100	98	99	102	110

Source: DfES (2002) Departmental annual report

therefore the natural accompaniment of the recent increase in funding. With more money, schools can create more posts. Consequently there is an increase in the demand for teachers, which translates into vacancies, which are likely to cause public alarm. Therefore, we are in the paradoxical situation that the recent crisis may be more the product of increased funding per pupil than of increased pupil numbers per se.

The age profile of full-time teachers in England and Wales in 2000 is shown in Figure 1.2. This pattern is the kind that leads some commentators to claim that the

Figure 1.2 *Number of full-time teachers by age group, England and Wales, March 2000*

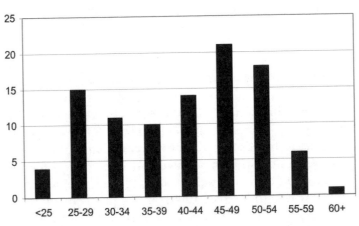

Source: DfES Database of Teacher Records.

teaching profession faces a longer-term crisis. They argue that once the cohorts currently aged 45 to 54 reach retirement age, the number of teachers aged 35 to 44 are insufficient to replace them. There is, in the words of one article, a ticking 'time bomb' (Howson 2001). However, there is nothing very special about March 2000. A very similar pattern of age cohorts appears in any year. What these commentators are doing is confusing the careers of the individuals represented in Figure 1.2 with historical cohort changes (see Gorard *et al.* 1999, 2002 for further explanation). Of course, the differences between age bands is related to the number of teachers available, which in turn is related to the number trained, the number of places available for training, and the number of pupils in any historical time period. The number may also be related to the economic conditions in each era following the initial training of most traditional-age students. But there are some constants in graphs like this from any recent year.

There are relatively few teachers under the age of 25, as only those individuals who enrolled on ITT courses almost immediately after leaving post-compulsory or higher education could attain QTS, and then be able to enter the profession before that age. Similarly, the retirement of women at age 60, early retirements, and increasing ill-health mean that bands from age 55 onward are also always very small. Shorn of these extremities, whatever the actual values are, the graph for any snapshot year shows this same dip in the 30 to 39 age bands. This age profile is, therefore, unlikely to be solely the product of historical trends in the recruitment of new entrants to the profession. An obvious plausible explanation for the observed pattern is teachers leaving the profession in their thirties. Indeed in 1999/00, 58 per cent of those who left or moved to part-time service were under 40 years of age, many of whom were women, themselves the majority of teachers, and not a few of whom can be expected to return to teaching at a later date (School Teachers' Review Body 2002). In five years' time there will probably be more teachers in the 40 to 44 age group than there are currently in the 35 to 39 group, when some of those leavers return after a career break.

Resignations by teachers in England and Wales rose from 25,170 in 1994 to 47,930 in 2001 (Employers' Organisation 2002). However, this does not mean that more teachers are leaving the profession, as the data includes those taking up employment in institutions similar to the ones they left. Most resignations are the result of people switching schools or moving to other LEAs. 'Natural' wastage due to retirement or maternity accounted for the next largest group. Total resignation and turnover rates can, thus, give a misleading impression of the state of the teaching profession. Those teachers moving from their present school to a similar one do not, presumably, present a major problem for the profession and cannot be reasonably considered as constituting 'wastage'. Retirements, whether due to ill-health or reaching the normal retirement age are usually unavoidable, as is maternity. It is only other types of resignation that can either be considered as a problem or become the subject of any strategies to increase retention in the teaching profession (Table 1.5).

One conclusion to be drawn from this re-consideration of existing data is that there was no especial crisis in teacher supply and demand in Wales (or indeed in England) at the turn of the century. The vacancy rate is now lower than in the past, and there are more teachers now than there ever have been, while pupil numbers are beginning to decline. Over the long-term and for the immediate future, the trend for pupil–teacher ratios is downward. The major limitation in the supply of new teachers is neither the availability nor quality of appli-

Table 1.5 *Destinations of LEA full-time permanent resigning teachers (1993–2001) who left education as a proportion of those who resigned (per cent)*

	1994	1995	1996	1997	1998	1999	2000	2001
Retirement	36	38	35	37	18	17	15	13
Other employment	3	3	3	4	6	6	5	4
Maternity	6	5	6	5	6	6	5	4
Other destinations	10	10	12	13	19	19	17	19
% left education	55	57	56	58	48	48	43	41

Source: Employers' Organisation (2002)

cants. It is the bounds set by recruitment targets to initial teacher training, and by the size of the overall graduate population, especially in maths and science.

If there is a problem, it is one of increasing demand rather than diminishing supply. Teacher shortages, when they do occur, are regional and may vary with subjects (and are exacerbated in Wales by the need for Welsh-speaking teachers). Some subjects and some types of school raise more difficulties than others. It is, however, difficult to decide on a precise level of teacher demand. It cannot be calculated simply using data on the number of teachers available and the number of pupils needing to be taught (Smithers and Robinson 1991). It is not clear that the vacancy rate represents much more than a snapshot of teacher turnover between schools, and when funding for teachers increases the vacancy rate tends to rise. Commentators deploring increases in vacancies are, therefore, often effectively deploring increases in the local funding made available to hire teachers. It is also possible for considerable teacher unemployment to coexist with vacant posts, as it does today. Pupil–teacher ratios are not much better as a simple indicator of teacher demand, because they cannot be simply converted to class sizes and they hide considerable regional and sectoral variation (and even variation between schools in some regions and sectors: McCreth *et al.* 2001).

Summary

This chapter introduces some of the ways in which everyday skill with numbers is also valuable for social science research. It suggests that, at this stage, researchers new to this area consider only a limited range of techniques that they are already mostly familiar with when shorn of technical mumbo-jumbo. These techniques involve simple figures, trends, tables, graphs, proportions, percentages, averages and average deviations. The chapter also presents an extended example drawn from real work that uses only these simple techniques, and which concerns itself more with the meaning and limitations of the figures involved than with complex analyses. The chief difficulty for anyone considering the possibility of conducting future work of this type, using everyday numeric approaches, is to overcome their belief that surely someone somewhere must already have made this simple consideration of patterns. As the teacher crisis example shows, it is clear that a lot of 'bread and butter' analyses remain to be done even on some of the basic relevant social science topics (at least in the field of education). The confidence to tackle such topics can really only come from un-learning some of the damage done by the usual methods-training for social science with its pretend paradigms and overly technical and unrealistic statistical techniques. Chapter 2 continues this un-learning process by considering the central question of how big a difference has to be before it is worth us trying to find an explanation for it.

2

Judgement with Everyday Numbers

'If your experiment needs statistics, you ought to have done a better experiment.'

Ernest Rutherford

Chapter 1 introduced some of the basic techniques for working with everyday numbers in research. This chapter continues a consideration of the fundamental research question of how large a difference has to be before it is worthy of attention. In doing so, it discusses the sources of error in numeric data, and several ways of re-phrasing numeric analyses to avoid misinterpretation. The chapter concludes with a second extended example of everyday techniques in practice in real research.

The Likely Sources of Error

Traditional statistical analyses are concerned only with sampling variation (sometimes called sampling error) stemming from the selection of cases at random from a population (see Chapter 3). They take *no* account of the multiple sources of genuine error that are a factor in everyday research situations. They take no account of the fact that the figures you are using are not entirely accurate (they are to the nearest unit of measurement, or as accurate as the measuring instrument will allow, for example). The figures contain an unknown level of measurement error. Many measures in common use in social science contain a very high proportion of such error. Think of attitude scales, the categorization of ethnic groups or occupational classes, the allocation of national examination grades, or definitions of poverty. What they all have in common is a high level of imprecision – some, like attitude scales, because of the vagueness of what is being measured, and some, like the allocation of national examination grades, because the size of the operation leads to mistakes and imperfect moderation between assessors.

In a sense, then, there are two distinct sources of error here. First, there may be a difference between the 'reality' you are measuring and the behaviour of the numbers you use as measures. If this difference is too great, then the act of measurement is actually bogus (pseudo-quantification). Second, there may be a difference between the measure you should assign to the reality using your chosen scale, and the measure you do assign. This is a simple mistake of the kind that we all make, especially when conducting repetitive tasks. While we can take steps to minimize the chance of such errors, we cannot guarantee their absence. One common source of simple mistakes comes from copying numbers, such as when transferring a list of numbers from paper to computer or calculator. Intriguingly, errors are also introduced merely by entering numbers into a computer or calculator even when the numbers are entered entirely correctly. A computer stores all its numbers in binary, and only allocates a specific number of binary digits to each number. The process of converting base ten numbers into binary numbers, therefore, automatically introduces small errors to some numbers, even where they start out as perfect representations of the reality you are measuring.

Another common, almost unavoidable, source of error comes from non-response. It does not matter whether the research is a small questionnaire survey conducted by a student, or the government's annual census of schools. For whatever reason there are always likely to be some cases that do not respond, or that do not respond in full. There is a very real danger that non-response leads to considerable bias in the results, if the non-responders are less literate individuals or busier schools, for example. These illustrations give some idea of the range of possible ways that genuine errors, completely unrelated to sampling variation, can creep in to our figures before we start any analysis.

Why do errors matter so much? Surely, we can just use the best available figures, analyse them accurately, and be aware that our results will not be perfectly accurate. Well – consider the following example. We calculate the mean score in a school test for a group of boys, and find the answer 60 per cent. We also calculate the mean for a group of girls, and find the answer 70 per cent. Let us imagine that both means are around 90 per cent accurate. An error component of one part in ten may seem reasonable when considering either figure in isolation. But this means that the boys' score actually lies between 54 per cent and 66 per cent (i.e. 60 plus or minus six). The girls' score lies between 63 and 77 (i.e. 70 plus or minus seven). If we subtract the girls' mean from the boys', the answer is ten. But the true answer could be anywhere between 23 (77 − 54) and −3 (63 − 66). Remember, these are not probability calculations, and the bands are not traditional confidence intervals (see Chapter 3). The difference −3 *is* as likely as any other answer. Therefore, despite both figures initially being 90 per cent accurate, when we subtract the two figures we genuinely have no idea whether the result is positive or negative. The error band for the answer, from −3 to 23 (or 26), is nearly three times the size of the surface answer (10).

This is worth emphasizing, since this 'propagation' of errors is not widely acknowledged in training texts, and because it remains completely neglected by traditional statistical analysis. Even where we have relatively accurate initial figures to work with, the process of conducting arithmetic with numbers changes the size of the error component relative to the numbers. Even such a simple technique as subtracting two numbers manages to convert an error of just one tenth to an error of 260 per cent of the figures involved. What has happened is that the initial numbers were so close that the subtraction makes them almost negligible in the result, leaving the answer to be made up almost entirely of error. This happens in all real-life calculations all the time. You may be able to imagine what happens to the error components in more complex analyses (see Gorard 2003a for a more complex worked example).

Two important points emerge from this consideration. There is no standard acceptable amount of error in any measurement. The relevance of the error component is a function of scale, and of the use to which the measurement is put. Also, the relative size of the error in any result is not determined solely by the accuracy of the original measurements. It depends on the precise steps in the ensuing computation. Of course, it helps if the initial readings are as accurate as possible, but whether they are accurate enough depends on what is done with the readings, and how the error component propagates as it is used in calculations. It is important to recall that every statistical, arithmetic or mathematical operation conducted with measurements is also conducted with their error components. If we square a variable, then we also square its error component and so on. The more complex the calculations we conduct, the harder it is to track the propagation of errors, even if we are aware of them at source, and so make an informed judgement of the ratio of error to final result. In extreme cases, the manipulation of variables leads to results almost entirely determined by the initial errors and very little influenced by the initial measurements. When answering a typical analytic question, such as 'is there a real difference between two figures', we need to take into account, in a way that traditional analysis ignores, the likely scale of any errors.

How Big Is a 'Difference', and Other Issues?

Imagine that we are trying to test the claim that someone is able mentally to influence the toss of a perfectly fair coin, so that it will land showing heads more than tails (or vice versa) by a very small amount. We might set up the test using our own set of standard coins selected from a larger set at random by observers, and ask the claimant to specify in advance whether it is heads or tails that will be most frequent. We would then need to conduct a very large number of coin tosses, because a small number would be subject to considerable 'random' variation. If, for example, there were 51 heads after 100 tosses the claimant might try to claim success even though the chance of such a result is quite high anyway. We could not say that 100 tosses would provide a definitive test of the claim. Imagine instead, then, one million trials yielding 51 per cent heads. We face at least three different types of explanation for this imbalance in heads and tails. First, this could still be an example of normal 'random' variation, although considerably less probable than in the first example. Second, this might be evidence of a slight bias in the experimental setup such as a bias in one or more coins, the tossing procedure, the readout or the recording of results. The key problem with such bias is that we have no reason to believe that its impact is random in nature. Third, this might be evidence that the claimant is correct: they *can* influence the result.

This situation, of facing three kinds of explanation, is one faced by all researchers using whatever methods, once their data collection and analysis is complete. The finding could have no substantive significance at all, being due to chance. It could be due to faults in the research, such as a selection effect in picking the coins. It could be a major discovery affecting our theoretical understanding of the world (i.e. that a person can influence events at a distance). Or it could be a combination of any of these. I consider each solution in turn.

An explanation of pure chance becomes less likely as the number of trials increases. In some research situations, such as coin tossing, we can calculate this decrease in likelihood precisely. In most research situations, however, the likelihood can only be an estimate. In all situations we can be certain of two things – that the chance explanation can never be discounted entirely (Gorard 2002b), and that its likelihood is mostly a function of the scale of the research. Where research is large in scale, repeatable, and conducted in different locations and so on, then it can be said to have minimized the chance element. In the example of one million coin tosses this chance element is very small (much less than the one in 20 threshold used in traditional statistical analysis), but it could still account for some of the observed difference.

Where our experiment has been constructed well, then the issue of bias is also minimized. There is a considerable literature on strategies to overcome bias and confounds as far as possible (e.g. Adair 1978, Cook and Campbell 1979). In our coin tossing example we could automate the tossing process, mint our own coins, not tell the researchers which of heads or tails was predicted to be higher, and so on. However, like the chance element, errors in conducting research can never be completely eliminated. There will be coins lost, coins bent, machines that malfunction, and so on. There can even be bias in recording, such as misreading heads for tails, or reading correctly but ticking the wrong column, and in calculating the results. As with the chance element, it is usually not possible to calculate the impact of these errors precisely (even on the rare occasion that the identity of any error is known). We can only estimate the scale of these errors and their potential direction of influence on the research. We are always left with the error component as a plausible explanation for any result or part of the result.

Therefore, to be convinced that the finding is a 'true' effect, and that a person can mentally influence a coin toss, we would need to decide that the difference that we have found is big enough for us to reasonably conclude that the chance and error components represent an insufficient explanation. Note that the chance and error components not only have to be insufficient in themselves, they also have to be insufficient in combination. In the coin tossing experiment, is 51 per cent heads in one million trials enough? The answer will be a matter of judgement. It should be an informed judgement, based on the best estimates of both chance and error, but it remains a judgement. The chance element has traditionally been considered in terms of null-hypothesis significance-testing and its derivatives, but this approach is seen as increasingly problematic, and anyway involves judgement (see below). But perhaps because it *appears* to have a technical solution, researchers have tended to concentrate on the chance element in practice and ignore the far more important components of error, and the judgements these entail. In fact, of course, what we need to aid our judgement is more data of a different kind. For example, we may want to use observation data from the experimental procedure. This is one more reason why experiments should always be seen as combined methods research designs (Gorard with Taylor 2004).

If the difference is judged a 'true' effect, so that a person can mentally influence a coin toss, we should also consider the importance of this finding. This importance has at least two elements. The immediate *practical* outcome is probably negligible. Apart from in 'artificial' gambling games, this level of influence on coin tossing would not make much difference. For example, it is unlikely to affect the choice of who bats first in a five-match cricket test series. If someone could guarantee odds of three to one in favour of heads on each toss then that would be different, and the difference over one million trials would be so great that there could be little doubt it was a true effect. On the other hand, even if the immediate practical importance is minor a true effect would involve many changes in our understanding of important areas of physics and biology. This would be important knowledge for its own sake, and might also lead to more usable examples of mental influence at a distance. In fact, this revolution in thinking would be so great that many observers would conclude that 51 per cent was not sufficient, even over one million trials. The finding makes so little immediate practical difference, but requires so much of an overhaul of existing 'knowledge', that it makes perfect sense to conclude that 51 per cent is consistent with merely chance and error.

'Effect' Sizes?

Are there, then, any simple rules we can apply to decide whether an apparent difference, pattern, change or trend in any dataset is actually worth pursuing? No. As the previous hypothetical example seeks to illustrate, we are always left with a judgement about the 'effect' and its size relative to the quality, scale and variability of numbers in which it exists. According to Cox (2001), the key issue is whether the direction of the effect is firmly established and of such magnitude as to make it of 'clinical' importance. We could posit a rule of thumb which is that we need to be sure that the effect sizes we continue to work with are substantial enough to be worth it. Clearly, this judgement depends on the variability of the phenomenon, its scale, and its relative costs and benefits. It also depends on the acknowledged ratio of effect to potential error. Therefore, a difference that is worth working with will usually be clear and obvious from a fairly simple inspection of the data. If we have to dredge deeply for any 'effect', then it is probably pathological to believe that anything useful will come out of it. We cannot specify the minimum size needed for an effect, nor can we use standardized tables of the meanings of effect sizes (Gorard 2006a). But we can say with some conviction that, in our present state of knowledge in social science, the harder it is to find the effect the harder it will be to find a use for the knowledge so generated. It is probably unethical to use public money pursuing some of the more 'pathological' findings of social science.

However, there are some relatively simple guidelines for analysis that will help our judgement and help prevent misrepresentation. If we focus for the present on trying to decide whether a difference between two sets of numbers is scientifically noteworthy, then there are two related issues that we can clear up before trying to make our judgements.

First, of course, we need to remain aware that a raw-score difference between any two numbers is heavily dependent on the size of the two numbers. A difference of one unit between a score of one and a score of two might mean rather more than a difference of one unit between a score of 1,001 and 1,002. This is well-known and understood in everyday situations. A score of 51 to 49 in basketball denotes a close game. A score of two to nil in football represents a reasonably comfortable victory margin. However, this distinction is regularly ignored in the more confusing environment of research, when it could be quite easily dealt with by looking at the differences in terms of proportions. For example, we could look at the differences in sports scores in terms of the total scores. Thus, a two–nil football score shows a 100 per cent victory margin, calculated as the difference in scores divided by the sum of the scores, or $(2 - 0)/(2 + 0)$, or 1. The basketball score, on the other hand, could be represented as a two per cent victory margin, or $(51 - 49)/(51 + 49)$, or 0.02. This simple conversion of the raw-score difference tells us what we should already know, which is that the football margin of victory is greater, but it does so in a formal, and standardized, way that can be used to guard against inadvertent misjudgement in the matter.

For example, when comparing the number of boys and girls who obtain a particular examination grade, we can subtract the score for boys from that of girls and then divide by the overall score. If we call the score for boys b and for girls g, then the 'achievement gap' can be defined as $(g - b)/(g + b)$. This is very closely related to a range of other useful measures and indices of inequality (see Taylor *et al.* 2000, Gorard and Taylor 2002). Of course, no such technique is perfect (see below). The role of judgement remains paramount. But not using one of these standard approaches has led many commentators into error and misunderstanding, about the apparent under-achievement of boys at school, for example (Gorard *et al.* 2001). If we have only the mean scores, then this is probably as good as our analysis can be (see next section).

Second, we might be able to describe any differences between two sets of numbers as scientifically trivial if the numbers themselves show considerable variation over time or place. Or, put the other way around, a difference between two sets of numbers is more convincing if the numbers themselves have a low mean deviation (see Chapter 1). As an imaginary example, consider two sets of ten numbers:

0, 0, 0, 0, 0, 0, 0, 0, 0, 0

and

2, 2, 2, 2, 2, 2, 2, 2, 2, 2

The sum of the first set is 0 and the sum of the second set is 20. Therefore, the mean of the first set is zero, and the mean of the second is 2. The mean deviation of both sets is zero, because there is no variability in either set. This makes the difference between the two sets startlingly clear.

Now consider another two sets of ten numbers:

15, 1, 0, −34, 1014, −78, 23, −345, −87, −509

and

15, 1, 0, −34, 1014, −78, 23, −345, −67, −509

The sum of the first set is zero and the sum of the second is 20. Therefore, the mean of the first set is zero, and the mean of the second is two. Using the proportionate difference between the means, as we did in the sports score example, would lead us to believe that the difference between the first two sets of numbers is of precisely the same size as the difference between the second two sets of numbers. However, everyday common sense tells us that the difference between the first two sets of numbers is quite clear. Every number in the first set (all zeroes) is smaller than every number in the second set (all two). The same common sense leads us to question the clarity of the difference in the second two sets of numbers. All of the numbers in both of the second sets are the same except for one. The difference between the two sets (20) is much less than the size of some of the numbers in both sets. Formalizing this common sense is one of the ways in which the mean deviation can help.

We can construct what is traditionally referred to as an 'effect' size by dividing the difference between two sets of numbers by their mean deviation. Traditional texts actually suggest using the much more complex standard deviation rather than the mean deviation (see Chapter 3), and they tend to be confusing about which standard deviation is used in practice (is it of one or both groups or of some other group like the 'population', for example). However, it is perfectly appropriate for the everyday analyst simply to standardize the mean scores by dividing each mean by its respective mean deviation, before calculating the difference between means.

Consider again the two sets of ten numbers:

15, 1, 0, −34, 1014, −78, 23, −345, −87, −509

and

15, 1, 0, −34, 1014, −78, 23, −345, −67, −509

The absolute deviations from their respective means (0 and 2) are:

15, 1, 0, 34, 1014, 78, 23, 345, 87, 509, giving a total of 2,106

and

13, 1, 2, 36, 1012, 80, 21, 347, 69, 511, giving a total of 2,092.

The mean deviation of the first is 2106/10 or 210.6. The mean divided by the mean deviation of the first set is 0/210.6 or 0. The mean divided by the mean deviation of the second set is 2/209.2 or 0.0096. Given that these figures are now 'standardized', the difference between them is rather small, or 0.0096. Put more simply, we should remain very sceptical of the apparent difference between the two sets of numbers because that difference is very small in comparison to the differences between the numbers within each set. This approach, of creating 'effect' sizes, is growing in popularity as a way of helping to assess the substantive importance of differences between scores, as opposed to assessing the less useful 'significance' of differences (Gorard 2006a). Where the individual numbers in each dataset are known, then this use of effect sizes is to be preferred to the simpler proportionate approach described above. However, like the proportionate approach, effect sizes are not a panacea and can be misleading. The role of judgement remains.

How Unfair Is an Inequality, and Related Questions?

As suggested above, work presenting numeric analyses routinely presents differences between groups over time or place without regard to the scale of the numbers in which the differences appear. And this is particularly problematic where percentages are involved. Imagine a social system with only two social classes, in which one per cent of social class A attend higher education (HE) while none of social class B do. In this society, therefore, all HE students come from class A, and to be born to class B means no chance at all of education at university. Now imagine a similar society with the same two classes, in which 50 per cent of social class A attend HE while 49 per cent of social class B do. Would it be true to say that equity between social classes is the same in both societies? Clearly not. But according to the government (at time of writing), most of the media and many academics, both of these societies are *precisely* equal in their equity of access to HE by social class. Their logic would be that the difference between the participation rates in the first society is one per cent $(1 - 0)$, and in the second society it is also one per cent $(50 - 49)$. This prevalent misunderstanding of the use of numbers when comparing changes over time or place between two or more groups has been termed the 'politicians' error' (Gorard 1999). Examples from all sectors of education appear in Gorard (2000a).

This 'politicians' error' appears, for example, in the DfES (2003) report 'Widening participation in higher education'. On page seven, the report presents a graph showing the participation rates in HE from 1960 to 2000 of two social groups – those created by collapsing social classes I, II and IIIN, and classes IIIM, IV, and V. In the year 2000, 48 per cent of the first group (non-manual) and 18 per cent of the second group (manual) attended HE as full-time traditional age students. In 1990, the figures had been around 37 per cent and 10 per cent respectively (Table 2.1) and the DfES describe this earlier position as better in terms of equality of access because $37 - 10$ is less than $48 - 18$. They even claim that 'if one turned the clock back to 1960 when there were just 200,000 full-time students, the gap between the two groups was actually less than it is now'. This claim is based on the fact that $27 - 4$ is less than $48 - 18$. Presumably, if the 1950 figures had been 22 per cent and 0 per cent, with no one from the less privileged group attending HE, then the DfES would describe this as even better in terms

Table 2.1 *Percentage participation by social class groups, England, 1960–2000*

Year	1960	1990	2000
Class I/II/IIIN	27	37	48
Class IIIM/IV/V	4	10	18

Source: DfES (2003)

of equity because $22 - 0$ is even lower than $27 - 4$. In fact, of course, none of these claims is justified by the data presented.

What the politicians' error does is to use a difference between two proportions with no regard to the size of the numbers involved (as though an increase of 10mph for a bicycle was the same as for a jet aircraft). Viewed proportionately, the situation in 2000 is more equal than in 1990, which is more equal than in 1960. A person in the manual group had around four and a half times as much chance of attending HE in 2000 as in 1960. A person in the non-manual group had only around one and three quarters times as much chance of attending HE in 2000 as in 1960. Or looked at in another way, the odds of going to university in 2000 were 2.7 times greater for social group I/II/IIIN than social group IIIM/IV/V, whereas in 1990 the odds had been 3.7, and in 1960 they had been 6.8. The situation was, therefore, better in terms of equity in 1990 than 1960 and better in 2000 than in 1990.

One of the consequences of the misunderstanding above is that other evidence relevant to widening participation is then misinterpreted. If, for example, a researcher or adviser genuinely believed that the figures in Table 2.1 showed increasing inequality of access by social class then they may conclude, wrongly, that a policy or practice that had actually been helpful was unhelpful or harmful. Even if a piece of research had been conducted as a rigorous trial of an intervention with appropriate controls, and the intervention had, in reality, been a success, a commentator may mistakenly decide that the intervention had been harmful because it purportedly widened the gap in access to HE by social class. The implications of this, once understood, are remarkable.

How do we overcome this problem? I have written elsewhere of several of the errors commonly made by social science researchers when trying to do calculations with percentages (e.g. Gorard 2003b). These errors and misunderstandings are crucial, because the risks and uncertain gains we work with in research are often probabilistic in nature, and are usually expressed as percentages. What I hope to do here is suggest one way of explaining, teaching and communicating the calculation of probabilities with minimal recourse to percentages. Insight into complex numeric situations can be encouraged simply by taking more care in the presentation of probabilities. Almost anyone can calculate conditional probabilities of the kind that would even confound some experienced mathematicians. To make this possible, we mostly need to change the way we think about and represent probabilities, rather than simply improve our own computational ability.

Imagine being faced with the following realistic problem to calculate:

> Around one per cent of children have a particular special educational need. If a child has the need, then they have a 90 per cent probability of obtaining a positive result from a diagnostic test. Those without the need have only a ten per cent probability of obtaining a positive result from the diagnostic test. If all children are tested, and a child you know has just obtained a positive result from the test, then what is the probability that they have this special need?

Faced with problems such as these, many people are unable to calculate a valid estimate of the risk. This inability applies to relevant professionals such as physicians, teachers and counsellors, as well as researchers (Gigerenzer 2002). Yet such a calculation is fundamental to the assessment of risk/gain in a multiplicity of real-life situations. What we need is an everyday solution to the problem, expressed in everyday terms.

Many people who offer a solution claim that the probability is around 90 per cent, and the most common justification for this is that the test is '90 per cent accurate'. These people have confused the conditional probability of someone having the special need given a positive test with the conditional probability of a positive test given that someone has the special need. As we shall see, the two values are completely different.

See what a difference a simplification can make. Consider exactly the same problem expressed in proportionate frequencies rather than as probabilities or percentages:

> Of 1,000 children chosen at random, on average ten have a particular special educational need. Of these ten children with the need, around nine will obtain a positive result in a diagnostic test. Of the 990 without the special need, around 99 will also obtain a positive test result. If all 1,000 children are tested, and a child you know is one of the 108 obtaining a positive result, what is the probability that they have the special need?

This is the same problem, with the same information as above. But by expressing it in frequencies for an imaginary 1,000 children we find that much of the computation has already been done for us. Many more people will now be able to see that the probability of having the special need given a positive test result is nothing like 90 per cent. Rather it is 9/108 or around eight per cent (see Table 2.2). While worrying for the child, eight per cent gives a very different prognosis to 90 per cent. Re-expressing the problem has not, presumably, changed the computation ability of readers, but has, I hope, changed the capability of many readers to see the solution, and the need to take a base rate (or comparator) into account for both steps of the calculation. This is far easier to compute

Table 2.2 *Probability of having a special need having tested positive*

	Test positive	Test negative	Total
SEN	9	1	10
Not SEN	99	891	990
Total	108	892	1000

Source: hypothetical

in simple frequencies rather than percentages. I realise that, even so, this is still somewhat confusing, and suggest that readers who do not find it clear try re-reading this section.

A similar generic problem involving misunderstood percentages concerns the use of symptoms in medical diagnosis (Dawes 2001). Imagine an illness that occurs in 20 per cent of the population, and has two frequent symptoms. Symptom A occurs in 18 per cent of the cases with this disease, and in two per cent of cases without the disease. Symptom B occurs in 58 per cent of the cases with the disease, and in 22 per cent of cases otherwise. Which symptom is the better predictor?

This situation is more complex than the previous example, because there are now two conditional probabilities to deal with. But the same approach of converting it into frequencies leads to greater understanding. Many practitioners would argue that symptom B is the more useful as it is more 'typical' of the disease. There is a 16 per cent gap (18 − 2) between having and not having the disease with symptom A, whereas the gap is 36 per cent (58 − 22) with symptom B. Symptom B, they will conclude, is the better predictor. But, while it seems counter-intuitive to say so, this analysis is quite wrong because it ignores the base rate of the actual frequency of the disease in the population.

Looked at in terms of frequencies, in a group of 1,000 people, on average 200 people (20 per cent) would have

Table 2.3 *Example of typical versus discriminating symptom*

	Illness	No illness	Total
Symptom A	36	16	52
Symptom B	116	176	292
Total with illness	200	800	1000

Source: hypothetical

the disease and 800 would not. Of the 200 with the disease, 36 (18 per cent) would have symptom A and 116 (58 per cent) would have symptom B. Of the 800 without the disease, 16 (two per cent) would have symptom A, while 176 (22 per cent) would have symptom B (Table 2.3). Thus, if we take a person at random from the 1,000 then someone with symptom A is 2.25 times as likely to have the disease as not (36/16), whereas someone with symptom B is only 0.66 times as likely to have the disease as not (116/176). Put another way, someone with symptom A is more likely to have the disease than not. Someone with symptom B, on the other hand, is more likely *not* to have the disease. What we need for diagnosis are discriminators, rather than typical symptoms. Simple differences between percentages give misleading, and potentially extremely harmful, results.

The ignorance of false positives in diagnosis, the abuse known as the prosecutor fallacy, the politician's error, missing comparators, pseudo-quantification and many other symptoms of societal innumeracy have real and sometimes tragic consequences. But confidence with probabilities *can* be improved. We can get better at dealing with probabilities simply by expressing them more naturally. What the examples in this section show, again, is that much of 'statistics', as traditionally taught, is of limited use in several areas of current social science research.

Discoveries Using Everyday Techniques 2: Is There a School Effect?

Here is a second real-life example of using everyday numeric techniques to reach useful research conclusions. It is based on a series of papers concerning the differential effectiveness of schools (e.g. Gorard 2005a, 2006b, 2006c). A concern for complex techniques of analysis and for the rhetorical sense of order imposed by allocating numbers to things has led an entire field of endeavour to miss the point that the results they generate are largely meaningless. Again, the use of a critical but everyday approach leads to a different conclusion, while more complex 'statistical' approaches lead us to apparent nonsense. The area of concern here is value-added analysis of school performance, and the fundamental error here, once accepted, has implications for policy-making, the local reputation of schools, and for studies of school effectiveness.

'League' tables of school examination outcomes have been controversial since their introduction in England and Wales in the early 1990s. In their simplest form, the tables list, alphabetically, the schools in each local education authority (LEA) area, the number of students in a relevant age cohort, and the percentage of those students attaining a level of qualification. In the printed press these tables have been presented in descending order of percentage attainment by schools. This information was intended to help parents and prospective parents to make judgements about the quality of their local schools.

However, these lists were labelled school 'performance' tables incorrectly, since it was clear that the percentage outcomes from each were heavily dependent on the prior attainment and SES background of the students in each school (Gorard and Smith 2004). In summary, schools near the top of such tables of outcomes also had superior inputs, in the form of already high-attaining students. It was, therefore, not at all clear how effective each school had been in producing the outcomes other than in attracting high-attaining students in the first place. In theory, it should be possible for some low-scoring schools to be more effective at dealing with equivalent students than some high-scoring ones, but for this not to be reflected in the raw-score tables. In response, such information is no longer made publicly available in Wales (or Scotland), largely because of its potential to mislead. In England, the alternative and perfectly rational response has been to try and maintain freedom of the information while remedying its defects.

The remedy has been termed 'value-added' analysis. In this, the prior attainment of each student is taken into account, such that the published figures reflect not the intake to the school but the progress made by students while in the school. The UK Department for Education and Skills (DfES) value-added scores for the average student progress from Key Stage 2 (the prior attainment of the student at primary school) to Key Stage 4 (examinations at the end of compulsory schooling) in each secondary school are calculated as follows (full details available at DfES 2005a). For the 2004 figures, all students in a school were included who were aged 15 or more on 31 August 2003, still on the school roll in January 2004, and with at least one matched KS2 score. The KS2 levels achieved by each student for each core subject were converted to point scores, and then averaged across the three (or fewer) subjects. KS4 points were calculated as a sum of the scores for the best eight GCSE results (or their 'equivalent'). Nationally, it is possible to calculate a middle value for progress from any KS2 score to KS4, such that half of the students make less progress and half make more. The median value for 21 points at KS2 ('equivalent' to an average of level three) was 202 KS4 points (roughly 'equivalent' to five GCSEs at grade C), for example. The value-added score for each student is the difference between their actual KS4 score and the median for their prior KS2 score. The value-added score for each school is the average of the value-added scores for all students meeting the definition above (with 1,000 added to this average to eliminate negative values). The results generally range from 900 to 1,100, but are not uniformly distributed. If this sounds complicated, that is because it is. The conversion of qualifications into points is especially problematic (see Chapter 3). To what extent is this complex analysis justified?

The re-consideration here uses the GCSE (KS4) results for mainstream secondary schools in England in 2004, their KS3 results for 2002, and the published DfES value-added scores for the same schools in 2004 (DfES 2005b). It is based on the 124 schools with complete information in York, Leeds, East Riding of Yorkshire, and North Yorkshire. These are used as illustrations of a wider pattern.

For the 124 mainstream secondary schools in the four Yorkshire LEAs, Figure 2.1 illustrates a cross-plot of the percentage of students in each school attaining five or more GCSEs at grades A*–C (the x-axis) and the DfES value-added score for that school. This shows quite clearly that schools with high outcome scores have high value-added and vice versa. There are no low to mid attaining schools with high value-added scores. Similarly there are no high to mid attaining schools with low value-added scores. In fact, we could predict the value-added figure for any school extremely well just from their absolute level of final attainment.

Note: The slight scatter at the 100 per cent end of the x-axis could be explained by the lack of freedom to vary at this ceiling. The schools at or near 100 per cent on the GCSE benchmark figure have some variation on the y-axis

Figure 2.1 *The relationship between value-added and absolute attainment 2004*

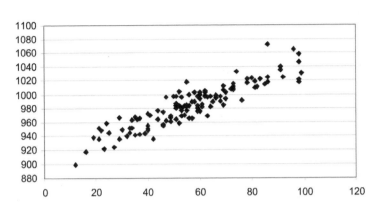

Source: DfES, www.dfes.gov.uk/performancetables

that is unrelated to the x-axis because that is the only kind of variation possible.

How can we explain this surprising pattern? It could, of course, be the case that the average progress made by students in all schools is truly in direct proportion to their school's average outcomes. After all, one would expect schools that helped students to make considerable progress also to have higher outcomes, in general, than those that did not. Perhaps Figure 2.1 merely reflects this? There are several reasons why this cannot account for all, or even much, of the story (see also Gorard 2006b). The pattern is too good. Given that the assessment system in England is not wholly reliable, and that no data collection, transcription, aggregation or analysis process is wholly accurate, this strong relationship between the DfES value-added figures and the raw-scores of absolute attainment suggests that they are both actually measuring the same thing. It would be, therefore, much simpler to use the raw-score values than to bother with the computation of 'value-added' figures that tell the same story. But these raw-scores have already been rejected by most commentators as being unrelated to school performance. This means, ironically, that the value-added scores have to be rejected on the same grounds.

Does which school a student attends, therefore, make any difference to the qualifications they attain? Put another way – is there a school 'effect'? It is clear that predictions of later examination scores are largely based on the pre-school and non-school context (Coleman *et al.* 1966, Gray and Wilcox 1995, Gorard 2000b). Once the individual student backgrounds have been taken into account, between 70 per cent and 100 per cent of the variation in student outcomes has usually been explained. The larger the sample used, and the more we know about each student, the higher the percentage explained (Shipman 1997). So, only between zero and 30 per cent of the student outcome scores could be explicable by the school effect. The size of this residual variation is related both to the scale of the study (small studies are more variable), and to the reliability of the measures involved (unreliable indicators generate spurious school effects, Tymms 2003a). In order to argue that *any* school effect actually exists, we would have to argue that this residual variation is so large that it cannot be due to chance or to errors (see start of the chapter). If so, we would need an alternative explanation and we could argue that the school effect is a good available alternative. On the other hand, we could argue that each student achieved pretty much as they would have done in any school, with any differences easily dwarfed by the likely error components. Which position we select is a matter of judgement, and must be based on a close examination of the many sources of error and an estimate of their impact relative to the residual variation.

It is clear that schools differ in terms of the proportions of their students achieving specified grades in public examination outcomes. It is also clear that these differences in outcome are related to the prior attainment, cognitive ability and socio-economic background of the students. Thus, a school with a student intake with high prior attainment, high cognitive ability and low levels of family poverty generally produces higher outcome scores than a school with an intake having low prior attainment, low cognitive ability or high levels of family poverty. If we take the nature of the student intake into account in a 'value-added' analysis, and there are still differences between schools, then we might be able to argue that the higher 'value-added' schools are more effective and vice versa. This would be a 'school effect', such that students attending a more effective school would score higher in the examination outcome than exactly equivalent students attending a less effective school.

In order to demonstrate the school effect we could set out to obtain comparable, reliable and valid outcome scores for each student. We would also need reliable and valid indicators of any individual characteristics that might influence those outcome scores, such as sex, age, ethnicity, family education, family occupation, prior attainment, cognitive ability, prior motivation, special educational needs and first language. We could use the latter to make the best possible prediction of the outcome score for each student, and then compare the predicted and actual scores in each school. If there are large and consistent differences between the predicted and actual scores for each school then we have demonstrated a plausible school effect.

Unfortunately, of course, neither of the premises in the above argument is realistic (Gorard 2001). We do not have comparable, reliable and valid outcome scores for students (Nuttall 1987, Newton 1997, Tymms 2003b). Nor, therefore, do we have comparable, reliable and valid prior attainment scores. We do not have reliable and valid indicators of even the most obvious background characteristics such as ethnicity, family education, family occupation, cognitive ability, prior motivation or special educational needs (Lee 2003). Allocating family members to occupational class schemes, for example, requires considerable judgement (Lambert 2002), and so introduces the potential for error. And we have no way of knowing whether we have included in our model *all* individual characteristics that might influence the outcome scores. Add to this the usual measurement, transcription, computational, propagated, non-response and drop-out errors prevalent in all research, and we can see that any school effect would have to be substantial in order for us to identify it over all that 'noise'.

The school effect may be simply an indication that we have not made sufficient allowance for one or more variables in our modelling of student progress. The primary school league tables in England for 2003, for example, were also intended to be value-added. However, most of the best-performing schools also had high raw-score attainment, and were sited in areas of relative advantage. Is this a fair result, or simply evidence that the value-added model was deficient, bearing in mind that 'school' performance was being judged on the progress of only around 30 to 60 students per school in terms of their 'expected' levels of attainment across different subjects, with all of the usual measurement and non-response bias?

Many studies find no school effect, including many of the largest and best regarded. The effect anyway disappears when non-cognitive dispositions, such as learner identities already possessed on entry to school, are included in the analysis (Gorard and Smith 2004). The view that performance at school is largely unrelated to any characteristics of the school other than the 'quality' of its students is quite widespread (Robertson and Symons 2004). Of course it is not actually possible to decide whether a student has progressed more or less in differing circumstances, because an individual cannot live two lives. Therefore, we cannot tell whether any school is more or less effective with the same students. Therefore, we cannot tell whether the difference between our best prediction and the final outcome stems from a fault in the prediction or is a real 'effect'. Knowing, as we do, how the assessment system works it is hard to see the residual variation as convincing evidence of the school effect.

If accepted, the figures above show that 'value-added' results for schools are nothing of the sort because they are not independent of the absolute level of attainment. The value-added figures are actually the *equivalent* of raw-scores and, therefore, suffer from precisely the same defects as raw-scores, of being largely predictable from prior attainment and/or student background. The rather lengthy procedures described by the DfES (2005a) to produce scores that are 'a measure of the progress students make between different stages of education' have been shown to be pointless. This may explain the otherwise rather perplexing finding from simulated models that value-added figures are no more accurate than raw-score figures as a predictor of school performance (Hoyle and Robinson 2003).

In fact, the value-added calculations are rather worse than pointless because their apparent precision and technical sophistication may have misled analysts, observers and commentators into concluding that they had succeeded, or that a greater range of variables or a more complex analytical model would somehow solve the outstanding problems. They make it harder for many commentators to understand fully what the figures mean, and what their limitations are. Some commentators will, therefore, become like one of the idealized 'villains' described at the start of Gorard (2003a), who are not appropriately sceptical of statistical analysis, and are overly impressed by technicalities at the expense of coherence and transparency. Policies concerning schools, and judgements about the relative effectiveness of different schools and types of school, will have been misled where they are based on the government's value-added analysis (or indeed any value-added analysis that does not correct the politician's error). Families may have been misled about the relative effectiveness of their local schools, with the schools in poorer areas and with academically weaker intakes suffering most from this misguided comparison dressed up as a 'fair test'. School improvers and school improvement researchers, relying on value-added analyses, will have been misled in their explanations and recommendations for practice.

Summary

This chapter completes the introduction to everyday techniques for dealing with numbers in research by considering how large a difference has to be before it is considered worthy of attention. It also considers some common problems in understanding inequalities and conditional probabilities that can be minimized by rephrasing the problems into more everyday terms. This is illustrated by a second extended example of important real-life research using only simple techniques. The next chapter lays out some of the defences that you may need when using everyday techniques and are challenged to use more complex approaches by traditional statisticians.

3

Defending the Use of Everyday Numbers

'Numbers are like people. Torture them enough and they will tell you anything.'

Anon.

Why is the advice given in this book up until now so different from the rules and procedures portrayed in traditional books on 'quantitative' research? The simple answer lies in the difference between reality (the world of everyday numbers) and the ideal universe inhabited by mathematicians. It is perfectly appropriate for a mathematician to make some imaginary assumptions, such that a set of data points would plot to form a perfect normal (Gaussian) distribution, or that they had been measured without error, and then work out the mathematical implications. This leads, among other things, to traditional statistics. But in the same way, it is perfectly appropriate (indeed advisable) for practical researchers to start from entirely different premises, such that any measurement could be in error, based on their experience of the real world. This leads to the kinds of everyday approaches to research with numbers described in this book. However, the hold of traditional statistics over *all* research with numbers – the 'quantitative paradigm' – is so great that some readers may want more than this simple answer, either for themselves or to convince their supervisors and mentors. Therefore, this final chapter presents in more detail some of the reasons why everyday approaches are actually more scientific than the heavily technical stuff usually presented to newcomers. As such, this chapter is a little more complex than the two preceding ones.

Not Four Levels of Measurement

One of the things that makes traditional statistics so complicated for newcomers from the outset is the theory that there are different 'levels' of measurement – usually termed ratio, interval, ordinal and nominal (see for example Siegel 1956). Books on statistics claim that we need to know about these four different kinds of numbers from the outset because their characteristics affect how we process or analyse them. But we do not learn about these four levels when learning to deal with everyday numbers, so what is the difference with numbers in research? Actually, there *is* no difference. It is perfectly possible to use everyday numbers in research without any reference to these supposed levels of measurement. For the kind of real issues we are concerned with in this book, there is only one type of number – a real number.

Both of what other commentators term 'ratio' and 'interval' measures are real numbers. Despite most texts and courses drawing the distinction between them because it supposedly affects how we analyse them, few of these commentators then ever go on to suggest that we treat ratio and interval values any differently in practice. This is because there is remarkably little practical difference between them. There are very few interval measures in reality (the frequently cited example of a temperature scale actually being the only one in common use, although rarely used in social science). The kinds of statistical procedures suggested for use with interval measures in traditional textbooks are identical to those for ratio measures anyway. The figures involved can be added, subtracted, multiplied and divided just like everyday numbers. The distinction seems only to make statistics more obscure for newcomers, and harder for most people to learn about. As becomes clear throughout this book, there are many examples of such apparently deliberate obfuscation in what are meant to be training resources.

So-called 'nominal' measures are, in fact, not numbers at all but categories of things that can be counted. The sex of an individual would, in traditional texts, be a nominal measure. But sex is clearly not a number – although each sex could be allocated a number for shorthand, just as different channels on our TV may be displayed as 01, 02, 03 etc. The only measure involved here is the frequency of individuals in each category of the variable 'sex' – i.e. how many females and how many males. Frequencies like this are real numbers, and they can be added, subtracted, multiplied and divided just like interval and ratio measures, and just like everyday numbers. Drawing a distinction between them, as is traditionally attempted, is largely pointless.

'Ordinal' measures are the basis of much nonsense in social science research. They are, at heart, simply categories of things that can be counted. In this way they are *identical* to nominal measures, and should be treated accordingly. Again, the identification of a different level of measurement is unnecessarily complex. The distinction is based on the claim that some sets of categories have an intrinsic order to them, and these are termed ordinal, whereas some categories do not, and these are termed nominal. The given example of an ordinal value might be the grades achieved in a school examination or test. But for everyday kinds of analysis, this order makes no difference beyond the obvious. In calculating the number of students achieving a certain grade or above, a teacher is not going to add in the frequencies of students below that grade, for example. It is also important to realize that an intrinsic order is available for just about any set of categories. The serial numbers for TV channels, treated above as a nominal value, could be placed in their order of appearance when flicking through with the channel 'advance' button, or the historical order in which they started broadcasting, or their transmission frequencies, and so on. These appear to be at least as well ordered as many social or occupational class categories that commentators try to order in terms of skill or prestige. Categories are not intrinsically either ordinal or nominal, and all can be described in either way without it making any difference to the everyday analysis involved.

The main reason why ordinal categories are treated separately in most books is that many analysts want to pretend that these are actually more like real numbers than they are like nominal categories. That is, analysts want to treat a numerical order of categories as though they were real numbers that can be added, subtracted, multiplied and divided in a normal way. They want to be able to claim that a grade 'A' in an examination is worth ten points and so five times as good as a grade 'E' scoring two points, for example. Therefore, if a grade B is worth eight points, then a grade A minus a grade E is a grade B, and so on (see the example of DfES value-added calculations in Chapter 2). Or they may want to claim that a person working in a skilled manual occupation is twice as skilled as someone working in a part-skilled occupation. This approach is very common in statistical work, but it is still complete nonsense. Categories such as examination grades, or occupational skills levels, are merely arbitrary thresholds superimposed onto theoretically continuous levels of variation. The difference in terms of marks or performance between two students with different grades in an exam could be less than the difference between two students with the same grades. Insofar as it is possible to decide how much skill is needed for a set of very different occupations – very problematic in itself – then it is possible for the most skilled occupation in the part-skilled category to be very close to the least skilled in the skilled manual category. The orders involved are not real numbers, and cannot and should not be treated as if they were. In everyday life, there is little confusion on this point. Only in traditional statistics is this confusion deliberately created, in order that analysts can convert exam grades to points, and then use a more convenient or more sophisticated analytic process which should only be available when they have real numbers. What these analysts are doing is sacrificing reality for technical obfuscation. In entering this fantasy land their losses as researchers clearly outweigh their gains, as illustrated throughout this book.

In summary, when working with everyday numbers in research or in real life, use your common sense but ignore the idea of 'levels' of measurement. If something is a real number then you can add it. If it is not a real number then it is not really any kind of number at all.

Not the Standard Deviation

Chapter 1 introduced the mean deviation (MD) as a measure of the variation around the mean within a set of numbers. This is simple to calculate, and as easy to understand as possible because it has an everyday meaning. However, the most commonly taught and used measure of such dispersion is actually the 'standard deviation'. It is obtained by summing the squared values of the deviation of each observation from the mean, dividing by one less than the total number of observations, and then taking the positive square root of the result. Using the same example as in Chapter 1, imagine that there are eight adults at a restaurant table, faced with a total bill in local currency of 80, of which each agrees to pay the average cost of 10. How fair is this if the actual cost of each person's meal was:

13, 10, 12, 11, 8, 6, 12, and 8?

To find the standard deviation, we take the deviation of each figure from the average:

3, 0, 2, 1, −2, −4, 2, and −2.

We square these to give:

9, 0, 4, 1, 4, 16, 4, and 4.

We add these together, and find that $9 + 0 + 4 + 1 + 4 + 16 + 4 + 4$ equals 42. We then divide this total by the number of people minus one. No, I am not clear why precisely 'minus one' is used here, and I suspect that no one else is either – it is an arbitrary adjustment for sampling error. This gives us $42 / 7 = 6$. We then take the positive square root of six, which is roughly +2.45. The main reason that the standard deviation (SD) was created like this was that the squaring eliminates all negative deviations, making the result easier to work with algebraically. Taking the square root at the end returns us to a value of the same order of magnitude as our original readings. The standard deviation does the same job as the mean deviation, but as I pointed out in Chapter 1 it is harder to calculate, and does not have a clear meaning, whereas the mean deviation is simply the average of all the differences. The standard deviation is also less tolerant of errors than the mean deviation, more closely tied to a specific distribution of figures (i.e. less generally applicable), and harder to relate to other simple everyday numeric techniques. By considering each of these points in turn, I wish to suggest that the mean deviation is both superior to, and easier to use for the same purpose than, the standard deviation traditionally taught to new researchers (see Gorard 2006d).

As early as 1914, the astronomer Eddington pointed out that 'in calculating the mean error of a series of observations it is preferable to use the simple mean residual irrespective of sign [i.e. MD] rather than the mean square residual [i.e. SD]' (Eddington 1914, p. 147). He had found, in practice, that the 'mean deviation' worked better with empirical data than SD, even though 'this is contrary to the advice of most textbooks; but it can be shown to be true' (p. 147). He also subsequently claimed that the majority of astronomers like him had found the same.

The statistician Fisher (1920) countered Eddington's empirical evidence with a mathematical argument that SD was more efficient than MD *under ideal circumstances*, and many commentators now accept that Fisher provided a complete defence of the use of SD (e.g. MacKenzie 1981, Aldrich 1997). Fisher had proposed that the quality of any statistic could be judged in terms of three characteristics. The statistic (e.g. MD or SD) for the sample and the actual statistic for the population should be 'consistent' (i.e. calculated in the same way for both sample and population). The statistic should be 'sufficient' in the sense of summarizing all of the relevant information to be gleaned from the sample about the population value. In addition, the statistic should be 'efficient' in the sense of having the smallest probable error as an estimate of the population value (parameter). Both SD and MD meet the first two criteria to the same extent. According to Fisher, it was in meeting the last criterion that SD proves superior. When drawing repeated large samples from a normally distributed population, the standard deviation of their individual mean deviations is 14 per cent higher than the standard deviations of their individual standard deviations (Stigler 1973). Thus, the SD of such a sample is a more consistent estimate of the SD for a population than MD is, and is considered better than its plausible alternatives as a way of estimating the standard deviation in a population using measurements from a sample (Hinton 1995, p. 50). That is the main reason why SD has subsequently been preferred, and why much of subsequent traditional statistical theory is based on it.

One further concern has been that the absolute value symbols necessary to create a formula for the mean deviation, by eliminating the plus and minus signs, are quite difficult to manipulate algebraically (http://infinity. sequoias.cc.ca.us/faculty/woodbury/Stats/Tutorial/Disp_ Var_Pop.htm). This makes the development of sophisticated forms of analysis more complicated than when using the standard deviation (http://mathworld. wolfram.com/MeanDeviation.html). So we now have a complex form of statistics based on SD (and its square – the variance) because SD is more efficient than MD under ideal circumstances, and because it is easier to manipulate algebraically. Of course, SD has now become a tradition, and much of the rest of the theory of statistical analysis rests on it (the definition of distributions, the calculation of effect sizes, analyses of variance, least squares regression, and so on). For example, SD is both based on and part of the definition of the widespread Gaussian or 'normal' distribution. This has the benefit that it enables commentators to state quite precisely the proportion of the distribution lying within each standard deviation from the mean. Therefore, much of the expertise of statisticians rests on the basis of using the standard deviation, and this expertise is what they try to pass on to novices.

On the other hand, it is possible to argue that the mean deviation is actually preferable and that, since Fisher, we have taken a wrong turn in our analytic history. The mean deviation is actually *more* efficient than the standard deviation in the realistic situation where some of the measurements are in error, it is more efficient for distributions other than perfect normal ones, and easier to understand. I discuss each of these in turn. However, we first have to consider what appears to be a tautology in claims that the standard deviation of a sample is a more stable estimate of the standard deviation of the population than the mean deviation is (e.g. Hinton 1995). We should not be comparing SD for a sample versus SD for a population with MD for a sample versus SD for a population. MD for a sample should be compared with the MD for a population, and Figure 3.1 (see below) shows why this is necessary – each value for MD can be associated with more than one SD and vice versa, giving an illusion of unreliability for MD when compared with SD.

Error Propagation

The standard deviation, by squaring the values concerned, gives us a distorted view of the amount of dispersion in our figures. The act of squaring makes each unit of distance from the mean exponentially (rather than additively) greater, and the act of square-rooting the sum of squares does not completely eliminate this bias. That is why, in the restaurant example, the standard deviation (2.45) is greater than the mean deviation (2), as SD emphasizes the larger deviations. Figure 3.1 shows a scatterplot of the matching mean and standard deviations for 255 sets of random numbers. Two things are noteworthy. SD is always greater than MD, but there is more than one possible SD for any MD value and vice versa.

Figure 3.1 *Comparison of mean and standard deviation for sets of random numbers*

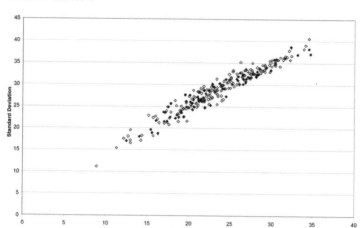

Note: this example was generated over 255 trials using sets of ten random numbers between zero and 100. The scatter effect and the overall curvilinear relationship, common to all such examples, are due to the sums of squares involved in computing SD.

Therefore, the two statistics are not measuring precisely the same thing. Therefore, the most important question is not which is the more reliable but which is measuring what we actually want to measure?

The apparent superiority of SD is not as clearly settled as is usually portrayed in texts. For example, the subsequent work of Tukey (1960) and others suggests that Eddington had been right, and Fisher unrealistic in at least one respect. Fisher's calculations of the relative efficiency of SD and MD depend on there being no errors *at all* in the observations. But for normal distributions with small contaminations in the data, 'the relative advantage of the sample standard deviation over the mean deviation which holds in the uncontaminated situation is dramatically reversed' (Barnett and Lewis

1978, p. 159). An error element as small as 0.2 per cent (e.g. two error points in 1,000 observations) completely reverses the advantage of SD over MD. So MD is actually more efficient in all lifelike situations where small errors *will* occur in observation and measurement (being over twice as efficient as SD when the error element is 5 per cent, for example). 'In practice we should certainly prefer d_n [i.e. MD] to s_n [i.e. SD]' (Huber 1981, p. 3).

Another important, but too often overlooked, assumption underlying the supposed superiority of SD is that it involves working with samples selected randomly from a fixed population (this is how its efficiency is calculated). However, there is a range of analytical situations where this is not so, such as when working with population figures, or with a non-probability sample, or even a probability sample with considerable non-response. In all of these everyday situations it is perfectly proper to calculate the variation in the figures involved, but without attempting to estimate a population SD. Therefore, in what are perhaps the majority of situations faced by practising social scientists, the supposed advantage of SD simply does not exist.

Distribution-free

In addition to an unrealistic assumption about error-free measurements, Fisher's logic also depends upon an ideal normal distribution for the data. What happens if the data are not perfectly normally distributed, or not normally distributed at all? It is quite clear that the advantage for SD only occurs with normal distributions. Fisher himself pointed out that MD is better for use with distributions other than the normal/Gaussian distribution (Stigler 1973). I have illustrated this for uniform distributions through the use of repeated simulations (Gorard 2006d).

But the normal distribution, like the notion of measurement without error, is anyway a mathematical artifice. In practice, scientists will be dealing with observations that merely resemble or approximate such an ideal. But strict normality was a basic assumption of Fisher's proof of the efficiency of SD. What Eddington had realized was that small deviations from normality, such as always occur in practice, have a considerable impact on *ideal* statistical procedures (Hampel 1997). In general, our observed distributions tend to be longer-tailed, having more extreme scores, than would be expected under ideal assumptions. Because we square the deviations from average to produce SD, but not MD, such longer-tailed distributions tend to 'explode' the variation in SD. The act of squaring makes each unit of distance from the mean exponentially (rather than additively) greater, and the act of square-rooting the sum of squares does not completely eliminate this bias. In practice, of course, this fact is often obscured by the widespread deletion of 'outliers' (Barnett and Lewis 1978). In fact, our use of SD rather than MD forms part of the pressure on analysts to ignore any extreme values.

The distortion caused by squaring deviations has led us to a culture in which students are routinely advised to remove or ignore valid measurements with large deviations because these unduly influence the final results. This is done regardless of their importance as data, and it means that we no longer allow our prior assumptions about distributions to be disturbed merely by the fact that they are not matched by the evidence. Good social science should treasure results that show an interesting gulf between theoretical analysis and actual observations. Extreme scores are important occurrences in a variety of natural and social phenomena, including city growth, income distribution, earthquakes, traffic jams, solar flares and avalanches. We cannot simply dismiss them. If we take them seriously, as a few commentators have, then we find that statistical techniques based on the standard deviation give misleading answers in these cases, and so 'concepts of variability, such as ... the absolute mean deviation, ... are more appropriate measures of variability for these distributions' (Fama 1963, p. 491).

Simplicity

In an earlier era of computation it seemed easier to find the square root of one figure rather than take the absolute values for a series of figures. This is no longer so, because the calculations are done by computer. The standard deviation now has several potential disadvantages compared to its plausible alternatives, and the key problem it has for new researchers is that it has no obvious intuitive meaning. The act of squaring before summing and then taking the square root after dividing means that the resulting figure appears strange. Indeed, it *is* strange, and its importance for subsequent numerical analysis usually has to be taken on trust. Given that both SD and MD do the same job, MD's relative simplicity of meaning is perhaps the most important reason for henceforth using and teaching the mean deviation rather than the more complex and less meaningful standard deviation. Most researchers wishing to provide a summary statistic of the dispersion in their findings generally do not want to manipulate *anything*, whether algebraically or otherwise. For these, and for most consumers of research evidence, using the mean deviation is more 'democratic'.

Therefore, even one of the first things taught on a statistics course, the standard deviation, is more complex than it need be, and is considered here as an example of how convenience for mathematical manipulation often overrides pragmatism in research methods. In those rare situations in which we obtain full response from a random sample with no measurement error and wish to estimate the dispersion in a perfect Gaussian population from the dispersion in our sample, then the standard deviation has been shown to be a more stable indicator of its equivalent in the population than the mean deviation has. Note that we can only calculate this via simulation, since in real-life research we would not know the actual population figure, else we would not be trying to estimate it via a sample. In essence, the claim made for the standard deviation is that we can compute a number (SD) from our observations that has a relatively consistent relationship with a number computed in the same way from the population figures. This claim, in itself, is of no great value. Reliability alone does not make that number of any valid use. For example, if the computation led to a *constant*, whatever figures were used, then there would be a perfectly consistent relationship between the parameters for the sample and population. But to what end? Surely the key issue is not how stable the statistic is, but whether it encapsulates what we want it to. Similarly, we should not use an inappropriate statistic simply because it makes complex algebra easier.

Of course, much of the rest of traditional statistics is now based on the standard deviation, but it is important to realise that it need not be. In fact, we seem to have placed our 'reliance in practice on isolated pieces of mathematical theory proved under unwarranted assumptions, [rather] than on empirical facts and observations' (Hampel 1997, p. 9). One result has been the creation since 1920 of methods for descriptive statistics that are more complex and less democratic than they need be. The lack of quantitative work and skill in social science is usually portrayed via a deficit model, and more researchers are exhorted to enhance their capacity to conduct such work. One of the key barriers, however, could be the unnecessary complexity of the methods themselves rather than any 'deficits' in their potential users. The standard deviation, like the four levels of measurement, is another example of such unwarranted complexity.

Not Significance Testing

The flagship of traditional statistics training in the UK is still the significance test. These are what generations of students have been taught, most have ignored, and many have abused. The classical form of statistical testing in common use today was derived from agricultural studies (Porter 1986). The tests were developed for one-off use, in situations where the measurement error was negligible, in order to allow researchers to estimate the probability that two random samples drawn (or allocated to groups) from the same population would have divergent measurements. In a roundabout way, this probability is then used to help decide whether the two samples actually come from two different populations. Vegetative reproduction can be used to create two colonies of what is effectively the same plant. One colony could be given an agricultural treatment, and the results (in terms of survival rates perhaps) compared between the two colonies. Statistical analysis helps us to estimate the probability that a sample of the results from each colony would diverge by the amount we actually observe, under the artificial assumption that the agricultural treatment had been ineffective and, therefore, that all variation comes from the sampling. If this probability is very small, we might conclude that the treatment appeared to have an effect. That is what significance tests are, and what they can do for us.

It is also important to emphasize what significance tests are not, and what they cannot do for us. Most simply, they do not make a decision for us. Standard limits for retaining or rejecting our null hypothesis of no difference between the two colonies, such as five per cent, have no mathematical or empirical relevance. They are arbitrary thresholds for decision-making. A host of factors might affect our confidence in the probability estimate, or the dangers of deciding wrongly in one way or another, including whether the study is likely to be replicated. Therefore, there can, and should, be no universal standard. Each case must be judged on its merits. However, it is also often the case that we do not need a significance test to help us decide this. In the agricultural example, if all the treated plants died and all the others survived (or vice versa) then we do not need a significance test to tell us that there is a very low probability that the treatment had no effect. If there were 1,000 plants in the sample for each colony, and one survived in the treated group, and only one died in the other group, then again a significance test would be superfluous. All that the test is doing is formalizing the estimates of relative probability that we make perfectly adequately anyway in everyday situations. Formal tests are really only needed when the decision is not clear-cut (for example where 600/1,000 survived in the treated group but only 550/1,000 survived in the control), and since they do not make the decision *for* us, they are of limited practical use even then. Above all, significance tests only estimate a specific kind of sampling error, but give no idea about the real practical importance of the difference we observe. A large enough sample can be used to reject almost any null hypothesis on the basis of a very small difference, or even a totally spurious one (Matthews 1998).

It is also important to re-emphasize that the probabilities generated by significance tests are based on probability samples (Skinner *et al.* 1989). They tell us the probability of a difference as large as we found, assuming that the *only* source of the difference between the two groups was the random nature of the sample. Fisher (who pioneered many of today's tests) was adamant that a random sample was required for such tests (Wainer and Robinson 2003): 'In non-probability sampling, since elements are chosen arbitrarily, there is no way to estimate the probability of any one element being included in the sample ... making it impossible either to estimate sampling variability or to identify possible bias' (*Statistics Canada* 2003, p. 1). If the researcher does not use a random sample then traditional statistics are of no use since the probabilities then become meaningless. Even the calculation of a reliability figure is predicated on a random sample. Researchers using significance tests with convenience, quota or snowball samples, for example, are making a key category mistake. Similarly, researchers using significance tests on populations (from official statistics perhaps) are generating meaningless probabilities. All of these researchers are relying on the false rhetoric of apparently precise probabilities, while abdicating their responsibility for making judgements about the value of their results. As Gene Glass put it, 'in spite of the fact that I have written stats texts and made money off of this stuff for some 25 years, I can't see any salvation for 90 per cent of what we do in inferential stats. If there is no *actual* probabilistic sampling (or randomization) of units from a defined population, then I can't see that standard errors (or t-test or F-tests or any of the rest) make any sense' (in Camilli 1996). Rather than modelling and inferential techniques, Glass recommends analysis via exploration and discovery (Robinson 2004).

Added to this is the problem that social scientists are not generally dealing with variables, such as plant survival rates, with minimal measurement error. In fact, many studies are based on latent variables of whose existence we cannot even be certain, let alone how to measure them (e.g. underlying attitudes). In agronomy there is often little difference between the substantive theory of interest and the statistical hypothesis (Meehl 1998), but in wider science, including social science, a statistical result is many steps away from a substantive result. Added to this are the problems of non-response and participant drop-out in social investigations, that also do not occur in the same way in agricultural applications. All of this means that the variation in observed measurements due to the chance factor of sampling (which is *all* that significance tests estimate) is generally far less than the potential variation due to other factors, such as measurement error (Sterne and Smith 2001, p. 230).

The probability from a test contains the unwritten proviso – assuming that the sample is random with full response, no dropout, and no measurement error. The number of social science studies meeting this proviso is very small indeed. To this must be added the caution that probabilities interact, and that most analyses in the ICT age are no longer one-offs. Analysts have been observed to conduct hundreds of tests, or try hundreds of models, with the same dataset. Most analysts also start each probability calculation as though nothing prior is known, whereas it may be more realistic and cumulative (and more efficient use of research funding) to build the results of previous work into new calculations (see below). Statistics is not, and should not be, reduced to a set of mechanical dichotomous decisions around a 'sacred' value such as five per cent.

The computational basis of significance testing is that we are interested in estimating the probability of observing what we actually observed, assuming that the artificial null hypothesis is correct. However, when explaining our findings there is a very strong temptation to imply that the resultant probability is actually an estimate of the likelihood of the null hypothesis being true given the data we observed (Wright 1999). Of course, the two values are very different, although it is possible to convert the former into the latter using Bayes' Theorem (Wainer and Robinson 2003). Unfortunately this conversion, of the 'probability of the data given the null hypothesis' into the more useful 'probability of the null hypothesis given the data', requires us to use an estimate of the probability of the null hypothesis being true irrespective of (or prior to) the data. In other words, Bayes' Theorem provides a way of adjusting our prior belief in the null hypothesis on the basis of new evidence (Gorard 2003b). But doing so entails a recognition that our posterior belief in the null hypothesis, however well-informed, now contains a substantial subjective component.

In summary, therefore, significance tests are based on unrealistic assumptions, giving them limited applicability in practice. They relate only to the assessment of the role of chance, tell us nothing about the impact of errors, and do not help decide whether any plausible substantive explanation is true. Even so, they require considerable judgement to use, and involve decisions that need to be explained and justified to any audience.

Suggested alternatives to significance tests include the use of confidence intervals and standard errors. But neither of these is a panacea for the problems outlined so far – chiefly the problem of estimating the relative size of the error component. They still only address the somewhat simpler but less realistic issue of estimating the variation due to random sampling. Confidence intervals and standard errors are based on the same artificial foundation as significance tests in assuming a probability-based sample with full response and no measurement error, and an ideal distribution of the data (de Vaus 2002). They are still inappropriate for use with both populations and nonrandom samples. Even for random samples, minor deviations from the ideal distribution of the data affect the confidence intervals derived from them in ways that have nothing to do with random error (Wright 2003). In addition, the cut-off points for confidence intervals are just as arbitrary as a five per cent threshold used in significance tests. In no way do they overcome the need for careful judgement. The major error component in our findings is not usually due to pure chance. Unfortunately the vagaries of pure chance are the *only* things that classical statistical analyses allow us to estimate (Gorard 2006a).

Not a Super-population

One of the ways in which traditional statistical commentators attempt to defend the general use of significance tests, even with population data, is to promote the idea of a 'super-population'. According to this model of enquiry, analysts are not, apparently, concerned to uncover specific patterns or trends, but to make more general claims about all possible universes, in which even data for an entire population is really only a sample from an infinitely large set of possible universes spanning space and time. Such a concept clearly has no relevance for everyday analysts, but some statisticians are forced by their advocacy of particular methods to assume that the data they work with are actually taken from these infinitely large super-populations. Goldstein, for example, argues that statisticians are not really interested in generalizing from a sample to a specified population but to an idealized super-population spanning space and time. In a debate on this matter, he claimed that 'social statisticians are pretty much forced to adopt the notion of a "super-population" when attempting to generalize the results of an analysis' (Camilli 1996, p. 7).

However, as Glass counters in the same debate, such imaginary populations are simply the evidence we have from the sample writ large, and necessarily having the same characteristics. This is the complete inverse of statistical inference, and makes any attempt to assess sampling errors erroneous. 'I think we're lost when we accept statistical inferences based on data that weren't observed, and moreover do not exist conceptually ... [Goldstein is] ... playing a game with the language' (Camilli 1996, p. 11). This kind of sophistry is retarding the progress of social science (Glass, commenting in Robinson 2004). To see how ludicrous Goldstein's suggestion is, recall the example of teacher numbers in Chapter 1. A policy-maker, concerned with the apparent crisis in UK teacher supply, might want to know whether the number of trained teachers was increasing or decreasing over time. They would want the best actual figures available for all recent years. They would not want to know how teacher numbers were changing in some imaginary universe spanning space and time. The super-population is a fascinating example of the outright nonsense that statisticians are led to when trying to defend their current complex practices. The only real purpose of the super-population is to provide an apparent justification for conducting significance tests on population data.

Not Multivariate Statistics

One of the most attractive facets of traditional statistics is the facility to create regression-type models. The new ESRC training guidelines mean that all new social science researchers should be able to conduct a multivariate statistical analysis, and the ESRC summer school is replete with courses on varieties of correlation and regression. Multivariate statistical analysis underpinned one of the key objectives of the ESRC's Teaching and Learning Research Programme (TLRP) Research Capacity Building Network (RCBN), and is a major component of the work of the ESRC National Research Methods Centre. Some disciplines, such as economics, and some fields, such as school effectiveness, are dominated by regression techniques. These techniques are useful, fascinating, and need to be clearly understood by a range of researchers, practitioners and policy-makers. However, like other techniques, they can give very misleading results and are, therefore, better used in combination with other methods.

If we create a table of random numbers in a statistical package, we can use this to test the discrimination of regression techniques (see Gorard 2005b). Imagine that this table has 20 rows each purporting to represent an individual's scores on 21 variables, themselves simulated by 21 columns of the random numbers. We can run a linear regression analysis with these 20 cases, using the first column to represent the 'dependent' (predicted) variable, and the other 20 columns to represent a set of 'independent' (predictor) variables. The analysis results in an effect size termed R-squared, which represents the extent to which the random values in the first column can be predicted using the random values in the next 20 columns.

With simple simultaneous entry of the predictor variables into the model (the default in SPSS), the resultant R-squared will always be 1.0 irrespective of the actual numbers involved. In standard reporting terms, this means that we will always be able to explain or predict all of the variation in our independent variable using our dependent variables – even though all of them are random and any relationship is, therefore, *completely* spurious. The same happens with a table of 40 rows and 41 columns, 100 rows and 101 columns, or of any similar shape and size. Of course, this peculiar result arises largely because there are as many independent variables as there are cases in the analysis. And this is why reputable texts emphasize that the number of cases in any study must outnumber the number of variables by an order of magnitude.

If we vary the analysis to use 'backward' elimination of any redundant variables, it is possible to reduce the number of independent variables in the model without substantially reducing the R-square value. In other words, we can still create a perfect prediction/explanation for the dependent variable, but this time using fewer variables than cases. And many of the variables retained will be listed in the output as 'significant' at the 0.05 level. If we are happy to allow the R-squared value to dip below 1.0 then the number of variables needed to predict the numbers in the first column can be reduced dramatically. Starting with a table of 40 rows and 41 columns it is easily possible, in this way, to produce a model with an R-value of 0.5 or higher using only ten or fewer variables for 40 cases. This R-value is higher than many of those that are published in journals, and that have been allowed to affect policy or practice. Many of these remaining variables will still be termed 'significant' by the software. And the ratio of cases to variables is 4:1, which can be considered reasonably healthy.

Perhaps you will think of this the next time you are about to be impressed by the R-value presented in a regression report. Try squaring the R-value, and then look at the result in terms of the ratio of cases to the variables actually used in the analysis. This last is often hard to establish from traditional reports. Once an investigation has started, the number of cases will usually only *decrease* from then on. There will be non-response and dropout from the designed sample. Many cases will have missing values for some variables. When these are excluded 'list-wise', the number of actual cases in the analysis can drop alarmingly. On the other hand, the number of variables involved often *increases* once the investigation is under way. The analysis could be run with one or more measures aggregated to different levels, or with measures combined with other variables to create new ones. Categorical variables are often converted to a series of dummy variables for linear regression, with one new variable for each of the categories (except one) in the original variable (watch out for this in research reports). A seven-point social class scale, for example, might be implemented using six separate variables. The upshot is that even the analyst may be unclear on the actual ratio of cases to variables used.

I have used simple linear regression in this explanation for clarity and familiarity, but the danger of spurious findings is a general one, and cannot be overcome by using alternative forms of regression. Similar arguments apply to logistic regression, or to multi-level modelling. In fact, more complex methods can make the situation worse, because they make it harder to establish how many cases (sampling units) there are. A good defence is, as always, to increase the number of cases and minimise the number of variables – because the problem of spurious patterns (the 'Bartlett effect') is, of course, even more likely when small-scale research is conducted in isolation. Another defence is to look at the same variables in another way, using a complementary method. This is one of the strengths of mixed methods work, wherein a tentative, theoretical, or statistical result can be tested by a field trial and/or in-depth observation, for example. A statistical result, such as provided by regression, is only the start of an investigation, not its end.

Complex statistical methods cannot be used post hoc to

overcome design problems or deficiencies in datasets. If all of the treated plants in the agricultural example on page 73 were placed on the lighter side of the greenhouse, with the control group on the other side, then the most sophisticated statistical analysis in the world could not do anything to overcome that bias. It is worth stating this precisely because of the 'capture' of funders by those pushing for more complex methods of probability-based traditional analysis (the post hoc dredging of sullen datasets), whereas of course, 'in general, the best designs require the *simplest* statistics' (Wright 2003, p. 130). Or as Ernest Rutherford bluntly pointed out, 'If your experiment needs statistics, you ought to have done a better experiment' (in Bailey 1967). Therefore, a more fruitful avenue for long-term progress would be the generation of better data, open to inspection through simpler and more transparent methods of accounting. Without adequate empirical information 'to attempt to calculate chances is to convert mere ignorance into dangerous error by clothing it in the garb of knowledge' (Mills 1843, in Porter 1986, pp. 82–83).

Judgement not Calculus

Perhaps one reason why research is not typically taught as an exercise in judgement is that judgement seems 'subjective' whereas computation is ostensibly 'objective'. This distinction is often used by commentators to try and reinforce the distinction between a 'qualitative' and a 'quantitative' mode of reasoning and researching. But, in fact, we all combine subjective estimates and objective calculations routinely and unproblematically. Imagine preparing for a catered party, such as a wedding reception. We may know how many invitations we send, and this is an objective number. We may know how much the catering will cost per plate, and this is another objective number. To calculate the cost of the party, we have to use the number invited to help us estimate the number who will attend, and this is a subjective judgement even when it is based on past experience of similar situations. We then multiply our estimate by the cost per plate to form an overall cost. The fact that one of the numbers is based on a judgement with which other analysts might disagree does not make the arithmetic any different, and the fact that we arrive at a precise answer does not make the final estimate any firmer. This last point is well known, yet when they conduct research many people behave as though it were not true. As we have seen, 'quantitative' researchers commonly eschew the kind of judgement at the heart of their decisions, seeking instead pseudo-technical ways of having the decisions taken out of their hands.

The standard ('frequentist') view of probability as used in nearly all statistics you will encounter is based on several premises, at least two of which can be challenged. Probabilities are assumed to be susceptible to objective measurement, and to have been calculated from scratch for each new problem as though nothing previous was known. Both assumptions are suspect. The first is almost certainly wrong in relation to social science, rather than games of chance. The second is also often wrong in practice, and clearly wasteful.

An alternative ('Bayesian') approach to probability is based on an acceptance that all 'knowledge' is subjective, and that all judgements of probability are therefore made on the basis of combining prior beliefs with new evidence. This is actually a return to the origin of modern statistical thinking in the seventeenth century. It was only in the twentieth century that statisticians, after Fisher, believed that probabilities were truly objective, and that 'significance testing' should proceed from the starting point of feigned total ignorance on any question. Our decision whether to play in the UK National Lottery, for example, is not based on the odds of winning alone (one in 14 million), otherwise *no one* would play. Rather we might take into account the more qualitative nature of the possible consequences (a loss of £1 compared to totally transforming our lives). Similar factors affect the decision to give a child the MMR (measles/mumps/rubella) vaccine or not (Matthews 2002). Bayesian probability is about how a person should decide, or bet (Hartigan 1983), and it shows that expected utility is subjective – the value of a bet can be subject to market forces for example (Gorard 1997). The wider relevance of freeing ourselves from the artificial assumption that numbers are inevitably objective can be seen, for example, in Gorard *et al.* 2004b.

At present, much of science is bedevilled by 'vanishing breakthroughs', in which apparently significant results cannot be engineered into a usable policy, practice or artefact. Epidemiology, in particular, and perhaps dietary advice, cancer treatment, genetics and drug development have become infamous for these vanishing breakthroughs. The traditional guidelines for significance tests, and the apparently standardized scales for effect sizes are producing too many results that literally disappear when scaled up. This book suggests that numeric analysis, in research as in everyday matters, should instead rely on judgement of the most personal and non-technical kind. Therefore, the key to reporting such analyses, and persuading others of our findings, is the clarification and discussion of those judgements and their (attempted) justifications. In this way, numeric analysis is no different from the analysis of other forms of data. Nor, as we have seen, is it very different from our everyday use of numbers.

References

Adair, J. (1973) *The Human Subject*, Boston: Little, Brown and Co.

Aldrich, J. (1997) 'R. A. Fisher and the making of maximum likelihood 1912–1922' in *Statistical Science*, 12, 3, 162–176.

Bailey, N. (1967) *The Mathematical Approach to Biology and Medicine*, New York: Wiley.

Barnett, V. and Lewis, T. (1978) *Outliers in Statistical Data*, Chichester: John Wiley and Sons.

BBC News (2001a) Why we left teaching?, http://news.bbc.co.uk/1/hi/education.

BBC News (2001b) Teacher shortages worst for decades, http://news.bbc.co.uk/1/hi/education.

Camilli, G. (1996) 'Standard errors in educational assessment: a policy analysis perspective' in *Education Policy Analysis Archives*, 4, 4.

Coleman, J., Campbell, E., Hobson, C., McPartland, J., Mood, A., Weinfield, F. and York, R. (1966) *Equality of Educational Opportunity*, Washington: US Government Printing Office.

Cook, T. and Campbell, D. (1979) *Quasi-experimentation: Design and Analysis Issues for Field Settings*, Chicago: Rand McNally.

Cox, D. (2001) 'Another comment on the role of statistical methods', *British Medical Journal*, 322, 231.

Dawes, R. (2001) *Everyday Irrationality*, Oxford: Westview Press.

de Vaus, D. (2002) *Analyzing Social Science Data: 50 Key Problems in Data Analysis*, London: Sage.

Dean, C. (2000) 'Anxiety mounts over staff shortage' in *Times Educational Supplement*, 30 June.

Dean, C. (2001) 'Staff crisis worsens as thousands quit: schools "haemorrhaging" teachers and recruitment cannot keep up' in *Times Educational Supplement*, 4 May.

DfES (2002) *Class Sizes and Pupil:Teacher Ratios in Schools in England*, London: HMSO.

DfES (2002) *Statistics of Education – Teachers in England*, London: The Stationery Office.

DfES (2003) *Widening Participation in Higher Education*, London: Department for Education and Skills.

DfES (2005a) Value-added Technical Information, www.dfes.gov.uk/performancetables/schools_04/sec3b.shtml (accessed 25/2/05).

DfES (2005b) www.dfes.gov.uk/performancetables (accessed 25/2/05).

Eddington, A. (1914) *Stellar Movements and the Structure of the Universe*, London: Macmillan.

Employers' Organisation (2002) *Employers' Evidence to the School Teachers' Review Body Concerning the 1 April 2003 Review of Pay and Conditions*, National Employers' Organisation for School Teachers, September 2002 (mimeo).

Fama, E. (1963) 'Mandelbrot and the stable Paretian hypothesis' in *Journal of Business*, pp. 420–29.

Fisher, R. (1920) 'A mathematical examination of the methods of determining the accuracy of observation by the mean error and the mean square error' in *Monthly Notes of the Royal Astronomical Society*, 80, 758–70.

Gigerenzer, G. (2002) *Reckoning with Risk*, London: Penguin.

Gorard, S. (1997) *School Choice in an Established Market*, Aldershot: Ashgate.

Gorard, S. (1999) 'Keeping a sense of proportion: the "politician's error" in analysing school outcomes' in *British Journal of Educational Studies*, 47, 3, 235–46.

Gorard, S. (2000a) *Education and Social Justice*, Cardiff: University of Wales Press.

Gorard, S. (2000b) ' "Underachievement" is still an ugly word: reconsidering the relative effectiveness of schools in England and Wales' in *Journal of Education Policy*, 15, 5, 559–73.

Gorard, S. (2001) 'International comparisons of school effectiveness: a second component of the "crisis account"?' in *Comparative Education*, 37, 3, 279–96.

Gorard, S. (2002a) 'Fostering scepticism: the importance of warranting claims' in *Evaluation and Research in Education*, 16, 3.

Gorard, S. (2002b) 'The role of causal models in education as a social science' in *Evaluation and Research in Education*, 16, 1, 51–65.

Gorard, S. (2003a) *Quantitative Methods in Social Sciences: The Role of Numbers Made Easy*, London: Continuum.

Gorard, S. (2003b) 'Understanding probabilities and reconsidering traditional research methods training' in *Sociological Research Online*, 8, 1, 12 pages.

Gorard, S. (2004a) 'Scepticism or clericalism? Theory as a barrier to combining methods' in *Journal of Educational Enquiry*, 5, 1, 1–21.

Gorard, S. (2004b) 'Three abuses of "theory": an engagement with Nash' in *Journal of Educational Enquiry*, 5, 2, 19–29.

Gorard, S. (2005a) 'Academies as the "future of schooling": is this an evidence-based policy?' in *Journal of Education Policy*, 20, 3, 369–77.

Gorard, S. (2005b) 'Is regression the way forward?' in *Building Research Capacity*, (forthcoming).

Gorard, S. (2006a) 'Towards a judgement-based statistical analysis' in *British Journal of Sociology of Education*, 53, 3.

Gorard, S. (2006b) 'Questioning the value of value-added league tables: the politician's error revisited' in *Educational Research*, (submitted).

Gorard, S. (2006c) 'Is there a school mix effect?' in *Educational Review*, 58, 1.

Gorard, S. (2006d) 'Revisiting a 90-year-old debate: the advantages of the mean deviation' in *The British Journal of Educational Studies*, (forthcoming).

Gorard, S. and Smith, E. (2004) 'What is "under-achievement" at school?' in *School Leadership and Management*, 24, 2, 205–25.

Gorard, S. and Taylor, C. (2002) 'What is segregation? A comparison of measures in terms of strong and weak compositional invariance' in *Sociology*, 36, 4, 875–95.

Gorard, S., with Taylor, C. (2004) *Combining Methods in Educational and Social Research*, London: Open University Press.

Gorard, S., Rees, G. and Fevre, R. (1999) 'Two dimensions of time: the changing social context of lifelong learning' in *Studies in the Education of Adults*, 31, 1, 35–48.

Gorard, S., Rees, G. and Salisbury, J. (2001) 'The differential attainment of boys and girls at school: investigating the patterns and their determinants' in *British Educational Research Journal*, 27, 2, 125–39.

Gorard, S., Rees, G. and Selwyn, N. (2002) 'The "conveyor belt effect": a re-assessment of the impact of National Targets for Lifelong Learning' in *Oxford Review of Education*, 28, 1, 75–89.

Gorard, S., Rushforth, K. and Taylor, C. (2004a) 'Is there a shortage of quantitative work in education research?' in *Oxford Review of Education*, 30, 3.

Gorard, S., Roberts, K. and Taylor, C. (2004b) 'What kind of creature is a design experiment?' in *British Educational Research Journal*, 30, 4, 575–90.

Gorard, S., See, BH., Smith, E. and White, P. (2006) *Strengthening the Teaching Workforce: Issues in Teacher Supply, Training, and Retention*, London: Continuum.

Gray, J. and Wilcox, B. (1995) *'Good School, Bad School' Evaluating Performance and Encouraging Improvement*, Buckingham: Open University Press.

Hampel, F. (1997) *Is Statistics Too Difficult?*, Research Report 81, Seminar fur Statistik, Eidgenossiche Technische Hochschule, Switzerland.

Hartigan, J. (1983) *Bayes Theory*, New York: Springer-Verlag.

Hinton., P. (1995) *Statistics Explained*, London: Routledge.

House of Commons Hansard Debates (2000) Teachers (Supply and Recruitment) 25 October, Column 287.

Howson, J. (2001) 'Young ones multiply' in *Times Educational Supplement*, 9 November.

Hoyle, R. and Robinson, J. (2003) 'League tables and school effectiveness: a mathematical model' in *Proceedings of the Royal Society of London B*, 270, 113–199.

Huber, P. (1981) *Robust Statistics*, New York: John Wiley and Sons.

Hutchins, L. (2001) 'Gloom of man who sent pupils home' in *Times Educational Supplement*, 23 March, 4.

Johnson, R. and Onwuegbuzie, A. (2004) 'Mixed methods research: a research paradigm whose time has come' in *Educational Researcher*, 33, 7, 14–26.

Lambert, P. (2002) 'Handling occupational information' in *Building Research Capacity*, 4, 9–12.

Lee, C. (2003) 'Why we need to re-think race and ethnicity in educational research' in *Educational Researcher*, 32, 5, 3–5.

Levenson, E. (2001) 'Recruiters frustrated as they are forced to appoint underqualified' in *Times Educational Supplement*, 25 May, 7.

MacKenzie, D. (1981) *Statistics in Britain 1865–1930*, Edinburgh: Edinburgh University Press.

Matthews, R. (1998) *Statistical Snake-oil: The Use and Abuse of Significance Tests in Science*, Working Paper 2/98, Cambridge: European Science and Environment Forum.

Matthews, R. (2002) 'The cold reality of probability theory' in *The Sunday Telegraph*, 5 May, 31.

McCreth, S., Menter, I., Hutchings, M. and Ross, A. (2001) 'Issues in Teacher Supply and Retention', presentation to Conference on Teacher Supply and Retention, University of North London, 12 June.

Meehl, P. (1998) 'The Power of Quantitative Thinking', speech delivered upon receipt of the James McKeen Cattell Fellow award at American Psychological Society, Washington DC, 23 May.

Murtonen, M. and Lehtinen, E. (2003) 'Difficulties experienced by education and sociology students in quantitative methods courses' in *Studies in Higher Education*, 28, 2, 171–85.

Newton, P. (1997) 'Measuring comparability of standards across subjects: why our statistical techniques do not make the grade' in *British Educational Research Journal*, 23, 4, 433–49.

Nuttall, D. (1987) 'The validity of assessments' in *European Journal of the Psychology of Education*, II, 2, 109–118.

OECD (2000) *Education at a Glance: OECD Indicators*. Centre for Educational Research and Innovation. Indication of educational systems.

Onwuegbuzie, A. and Wilson, V. (2003) 'Statistics anxiety: nature, etiology, antecedents, effects and treatments – a comprehensive review of the literature' in *Teaching in Higher Education*, 8, 2, 195–209.

Phillips, D. (1999) 'How to play the game: a Popperian approach to the conduct of research' in: G. Zecha (ed.) *Critical Rationalism and Educational Discourse*, Amsterdam: Rodopi.

Porter, T. (1986) *The Rise of Statistical Thinking*, Princeton: Princeton University Press.

Rendall, M. (2003) *Quantitative Research: A Scoping Study*, London: Learning and Skills Research Centre.

Report of Sir Gareth Roberts' Review (2002) *SET for Success: The Supply of People with Science, Technology and Mathematics Skills*, April 2002.

Robertson, D. and Symons, J. (2004) 'Self-selection in the state school system' in *Education Economics*, 11, 3, 259–272.

Robinson, D. (2004) 'An interview with Gene Glass' in *Educational Researcher*, 33, 3, 26–30.

School Teachers' Review Body (2000) *Written Evidence from the Department for Education and Employment: Statistical Annex*, London: The Stationery Office.

School Teachers' Review Body (2001) *Tenth Report*, London: The Stationery Office.

School Teachers' Review Body (2002) *Eleventh Report*, London: The Stationery Office.

Schoolsnet (2001) 'Paradox lost' in *Educational Journal*. 56, 1 January.

See, BH., Gorard, S. and White, P. (2004) 'Teacher demand: crisis, what crisis?' in *Cambridge Journal of Education*, 34, 1, 103–123.

Shipman, M. (1997) *The Limitations of Social Research*, Harlow: Longman.

Shvyrkov, V. (1997) 'The new statistical thinking' in *Quality and Quantity*, 31, 155–171.

Siegel, S. (1956) *Nonparametric Statistics*, Tokyo: McGraw-Hill.

Skinner, C., Holt, D. and Smith, T. (1989) *Analysis of Complex Surveys*, Chichester: John Wiley and Sons.

Smithers, A. and Robinson, P. (1990) *Teacher Provision: Trends and Perceptions*, Manchester: School of Education.

Smithers, R. (2001a) 'Teacher job crisis on eve of new school year' in *The Guardian*, 30 August, 1.

Smithers, R. (2001b) 'Foreign recruits hit record numbers' in *Times Educational Supplement*, 30 August, 4.

Statistics Canada (2003) *Non-probability Sampling*, www. statcan.ca/english/power/ch13/ (accessed 5/1/04).

Sterne, J. and Smith, G. (2001) 'Sifting the evidence – what's wrong with significance tests' in *British Medical Journal*, 322, 226–31.

Stigler, S. (1973) 'Studies in the history of probability and statistics XXXII: Laplace, Fisher and the discovery of the concept of sufficiency' in *Biometrika*, 60, 3, 439–45.

Taylor, C., Gorard, S. and Fitz, J. (2000) 'A re-examination of segregation indices in terms of compositional invariance' in *Social Research Update*, 30, 1–4.

TES (2002) 'Crisis? What crisis?' in *Times Educational Supplement.* 1 November, 26.

Tukey, J. (1960) 'A survey of sampling from contaminated distributions' in Olkin, I., Ghurye, S., Hoeffding, W., Madow, W and Mann, H. (eds.) *Contributions to Probability and Statistics: Essays in Honor of Harold Hotelling*, Stanford: Stanford University Press.

Tymms, P. (2003a) 'School Composition Effects', School of Education, Durham University, January 2003.

Tymms, P. (2003b) 'Standards Over Time', presentation at BERA annual conference, September 2003, Edinburgh.

Wainer, H. and Robinson, D. (2003) 'Shaping up the practice of null hypothesis significance testing' in *Educational Researcher*, 32, 7, 22–30.

White, P., Gorard, S. and See, BH. (2005) 'What are the problems with teacher supply?' in *Teachers and Teacher Education*, (forthcoming).

Woodward, W. (2001) 'Four day week threat to pupils' in *Times Educational Supplement*, 22 June, 13.

Wright, D. (1999) 'Science, statistics and the three "psychologies"' in Dorling, D. and Simpson, L. (eds) *Statistics in Society*, London: Arnold.

Wright, D. (2003) 'Making friends with your data: improving how statistics are conducted and reported' in *British Journal of Educational Psychology*, 73, 123–36.